Identifying Additional Learning Needs

'I know there is something wrong, but what?'
'How do I know if outside help for this child is needed?'

These are questions that most nursery workers will have to face at some stage in their careers. In this highly informative book, Christine Macintyre urges practitioners to spot indications of possible special needs by *listening* to the young children in their care. She shows that through active listening and watching, a valuable 'child's-eye view' of the world can be understood.

This book uses a case study approach, giving many examples of children's experiences and the support strategies that were found to help them. Interactions with parents are shared too, to help practitioners understand how the children's difficulties affect them at home. In addition, the book explores:

- ▶ the process of early identification;
- ▶ communication between parents and nursery staff;
- ▶ how to spot early indications of key difficulties, such as dyspraxia, dyslexia and autism;
- ▶ how parents, professionals and the children themselves can work together to maximise opportunities for learning.

Early-years practitioners and students will find this an indispensable guide.

Christine Macintyre is a Fellow of Edinbugh University. She lectured there in Child Development, Play and Special Needs, and currently offers training in all aspects of development in the Early Years.

The Nursery World/Routledge
Essential Guides for Early Years Practitioners

Books in this series address key issues for early years practitioners working in today's nursery and school environments. Each title is packed full of practical activities, support, advice and guidance, all of which is in line with current government early years policy. The authors use their experience and expertise to write accessibly and informatively, emphasising through the use of case studies the practical aspects of the subject, whilst retaining strong theoretical underpinnings throughout.

These titles will encourage the practitioner and student alike to gain greater confidence and authority in their day-to-day work, offering many illustrative examples of good practice, suggestions for further reading and many invaluable resources. For a handy, clear and inspirational guide to understanding the important and practical issues, the early years practitioner or student need look no further then this series.

Titles in the series:

Circle Time for Young Children
Jenny Mosley

Helping with Behaviour
Sue Roffey

Identifying Additional Learning Needs: listening to the children
Christine Macintyre

Observing, Assessing and Planning for Children in the Early Years
Sandra Smidt

Encouraging Creative Play and Learning (forthcoming)
Diane Rich

Identifying Additional Learning Needs

Listening to the children

Christine Macintyre

 Routledge
Taylor & Francis Group

LONDON AND NEW YORK

NURSERY
WORLD

First published 2005
by Routledge
2 Park Square, Milton Park, Abingdon, Oxon OX14 4RN

Simultaneously published in the USA and Canada
by Routledge
270 Madison Ave, New York, NY 10016

Routledge is an imprint of the Taylor & Francis Group

Typeset in Perpetua and Bell Gothic
by Florence Production Ltd, Stoodleigh, Devon
Printed and bound in Great Britain by
TJ International Ltd, Padstow, Cornwall

Key Guides for Effective Teaching in Higher Education web resource

The Key Guides for Effective Teaching in Higher Education Series
provides guidance and advice for those looking to improve their
teaching and learning. It is accompanied by a useful website which
features brand new supplementary material, including How Students
Learn, a guide written by Professor George Brown which provides
outlines and commentaries on theories of learning and their
implications for teaching practice.

Visit the website at:
http://www.routledgefalmer.com/series/KGETHE

The Routledge website also features a wide range of books for
lecturers and higher education professionals

British Library Cataloguing in Publication Data
A catalogue record for this book is available from
the British Library

Library of Congress Cataloging in Publication Data
A catalog record for this book has been requested

ISBN 0–415–36214–8 (hbk)
ISBN 0–415–36215–6 (pbk)

Contents

PART III
Overview

Illustrations

FIGURES

TABLES

Acknowledgements

There are many people who have made this book possible, and I should like to thank them all. First, thanks are due to the Carnegie Trust (Scotland), who funded the research and made 'asking the children' possible. Thank you too to all the parents who were so generous in sharing their time and their experiences. Having a child with difficulties, whether mild or profound, is hugely emotional and time-consuming, yet they were willing to explain their child's particular pattern of problems and share their expertise in reducing them. They also gave permission for these to be shared in the hope that strategies that helped their child could benefit others too. Sincere thanks also to the nursery practitioners. They had many demands on their time, yet they were anxious to try out observations and assessments and to analyse the things the children said. They were genuine partners in the research. Many found that 'really listening to the children gave us insights we've never had before' and that 'listening and encouraging the children to share their views helped us to build a special kind of relationship – one in which we took time to appreciate the hazards of learning from the child's point of view'. My best thanks go to them all.

Part I

Identifying difficulties

The importance of communication

Chapter 1

The early identification of learning difficulties

When young children come into nursery, they enter a welcoming, caring environment where practitioners specially trained in the development of early-years children provide a colourful, stimulating environment for learning. Many children are intrigued and entranced, and immediately investigate the resources and the people who are there to help them. Other children are more reluctant to join in but soon overcome their initial hesitation, and they and their parents can relax. All is well. Sadly, another, and increasingly large, group of children are not able to settle down and make the most of their time there.

In nursery, most children are considered to be too young to have a 'label' indicating a learning difficulty, because maturation, experience and careful teaching may offset early concerns. Nonetheless, nursery staff must be observing and assessing the acquisition of all the early competences so that they can support the children in the most appropriate way. If specific learning difficulties or any other additional need is already present or appears to be looming, then positive intervention cannot be delayed. This input may well overcome any barriers to learning. Early diagnosis does not mean that a 'label' is inevitable. But where difficulties persist, nursery staff (in collaboration with special educational needs co-ordinators (SENCOs) or line managers) have to seek referral to the appropriate specialists, wherever possible presenting evidence of their claims. (Different regions have their own procedures and channels of communication for doing this, and these have to be carefully followed.)

What difficulties are very young children likely to display?

▶   Children with a range of difficulties – primarily social and emotional difficulties, primarily intellectual difficulties,

primarily motor (movement) difficulties or a blend of all three
– find they are not able to cope with the busyness of the new
environment. This has more children moving around in a bigger,
livelier space than they have ever encountered before.

These children need a great deal of time and extra support to help
them acclimatise to a new, very different environment. The colour of
pictures on the wall, the lightness of the room, the variety of resources
and the constant movement of the other small people and the group of
unknown adults can distress some children and be overwhelming for
those who are even marginally on the autistic spectrum. Some sensitive, vulnerable children with poor spatial awareness (one element of
dyspraxia and dyslexia) can be genuinely frightened by lively children
who might (in their eyes) hurt them. The other children may just
come too close, but to children who cannot bear anyone to intrude on
their personal space, they appear aggressive. In the earliest days some
children will not realise that adults are there to support and protect
them. This lack of understanding can be exacerbated if they cannot
speak clearly, for then they are hampered by being unable to make their
feelings known.

Another group of children – those who find it difficult to be still,
or those who are impulsive (possible symptoms of the attention disorders ADD and ADHD (attention deficit disorder and attention deficit
hyperactivity disorder) – can find waiting for a turn or being quiet at
story time really hard. And others may anticipate not being able to make
a friend or join in a game or climb on the climbing frame and, feeling
inadequate or insecure, would really prefer to go home. Children have
very different temperaments, strengths and limitations, and these influence how they welcome or reject new challenges. Add to that any of
the learning difficulties or global developmental delay that may be part
of their make-up and it can be seen that going to nursery or school
may not be such a straightforward happening after all.

▶ Some children may be unable to play (either at all, or
appropriately for their chronological age).

Children pass through developmental stages in their play (see Table 1.1)
just as they do in other aspects of their learning. By the time they come
to nursery, most children will play alongside others happily (i.e. engage
in parallel play), even although they may not interact a great deal. Soon

TABLE 1.1 The developmental stages of play

Stages of play	Age (years)	Characteristics
Sensorimotor play (manipulation of objects)	0–2	Holding, sucking, dropping and retrieving objects; investigating their literal properties, i.e. without pretence
Constructive play	2+	Beginning to use two objects to form another, e.g. build bricks, put car in garage or doll in pram
Pretend play – also called fantasy or imaginative play	3–7	Pretending a toy is something else, e.g. a yo-yo is a dog on a lead Having an imaginary friend
Socio-dramatic play	4+	Role play – acting out the characteristics of another person
Games with rules	7+	Following instructions, e.g. in a board game; coping with the change of ends in ball games; following the plot in imaginary play

they are able to share resources and, through that, come to chat over ideas and make plans. They become able to take turns and are willing to wait and allow someone else to have a turn. They have developed empathy (i.e. the understanding that others have feelings and ideas, and the ability to recognise and take account of them). Intermittent squabbles notwithstanding, they have moved from parallel play to interactive play to imaginative play, perhaps taking on the role of another person.

But children with additional needs may not be able to follow this usual progression. Empathy, the source of apt communication, does not develop well in children on the autistic spectrum. Those with dyspraxia may not have the muscle strength or co-ordination to allow them to participate in climbing or crawling games, or they may not be able to handle jigsaws or toys with care and are often blamed for spoiling the game. Even at nursery (although this is more marked at primary school), children can be quick to evaluate the prowess of others, so children with poor ball skills get left out of popular outdoor games. This does their self-esteem no good at all.

Many children with organising and planning difficulties – for example, those found in dyslexia, dyspraxia, ADHD and Asperger's syndrome –

5

may be defeated by the implicit sequencing of events within play scenarios that somehow have to be understood without explanations of why they are occurring. And children with the attention deficit disorders may in addition not have the concentration to wait to follow the unwritten rules of a game. For some children, playtime is not the happy social event it is supposed to be.

► Children come with 'baggage'. When they arrive at nursery or school they have already developed ways of behaving based on interacting with their models – that is, the familiar adults and children they have seen.

All children are influenced by their home background, whatever that might be, and early-years practitioners have to appreciate the advantages and limitations of different contexts and how they impinge on a child's ability to learn. This is not easy, because a child's home could have very different values and viewpoints from those seen as important in nursery or school. This is an environmental or nurture effect that can cause children to be either confident and competent or confused, uneasy or rebellious in new surroundings. Moreover, a great danger lurks here, namely that inexperienced practitioners will make assumptions that are not true. This happens when knowledge of a child's background colours the expectations and the assessment of that particular child. Children from a severely disadvantaged background or with older siblings who have been troublemakers or with parents who have pushed for their children to be noticed or been uncommunicative with staff, need to be welcomed openly and not carry the baggage of their 'other life'.

In 2004, Peter Peacock, the Education Minister, advised schools to have much more contact with parents so that they could continue their children's education at home. Some teachers might well argue that where this is a good thing it is happening already, as many parents support the nursery school in a range of ways, such as by preparing resources in the nursery or helping with baking, as well as supporting the children at home, perhaps by sharing stories from the story sacs or just ensuring that they arrive on time, fresh and ready to learn. (A story sac is a bag containing a book and a toy and/or some related article to expand the child's understanding and stimulate learning. It can be taken home so that child and parents can share the contents.) If this sort of involvement doesn't happen, however, there could be a multitude of practical or educational reasons why parents can't become involved. They may be working or supporting elderly relatives; they may be disabled themselves and find travelling to school impossible; they may feel inadequate in terms of not understanding modern education and recognise that their ideas about what happens in schools are no longer relevant. They may even consider that they are to blame for their children's difficulties and be afraid to find out more.

But when there are children with additional learning needs, it surely makes sense that all the carers have the same learning goals and understand the way the nursery promotes them – that is, through play activities – because differences can confuse the children and make their learning more difficult than it need be. Moreover there are research findings, such as those from the Family Numeracy project (1998), suggesting that where parents and children are given support together, the parents are likely to keep helping their children and are 'twice as likely to be involved in their child's school'. Most nurseries would not have the staff to teach parents as well as the children, but encouraging parents to come into the nursery and/or explaining its goals can give parents who cannot read English a chance to learn through osmosis. Others can borrow books such as *Planning the Pre-5 Setting*, or the specialist magazine *Nursery World*, depending on how much they wish to know.

► Children have an inbuilt set of skills and abilities that are more or less amenable to change.

The extent to which these 'fit' the accepted mode of learning in nursery and the need for them to be extended or amended by the staff there is a complex one, often dependent on the prevailing ethos of what is 'right' or 'best for the child'. Many moral issues must be considered here. Does education in nursery and school exist to make each child fit the mould or should individual differences be nurtured to give a more colourful and empathetic group? Even the question of giving 'rewards' begs the question 'Do I need you to do this more than you want to do it yourself?', and is this move, often called a positive reinforcement strategy, really a hidden agenda to promote conformity? Against that stance, of course, is the premise that thirty or so children can't all do what they like when they like, but the argument is worth considering.

In schools, 'golden time' is very often given as a reward, implicitly suggesting that the activities therein are 'better' than work. Should the work not be so interesting and valuable so that it becomes the thing that is most important? Considerations like this conjure up the issue of intervention. Questions of whether to intervene or not, and how or when to do it, are a constant source of discussion and debate. When children have special needs, the question is even more complex, as opportunities to be resourceful and imaginative and to think beyond everyday coping issues are extremely important for the children's self-esteem and future independence.

▶ The scope of intervention

In recent years, early intervention has been the key phrase in supporting children with additional learning needs or from disadvantaged homes. But how have these children been identified and what process has been followed? At what age did intervention begin and for how long was the intervention sustained? And did the initial advantage last once the special programme was withdrawn? In some regions, a paucity of resources has meant that only the most needy children have access to specialist help, while borderline cases have to go without.

In practice, there can be children not disabled enough for special school but not able to cope with the work in specialist language units (nursery teacher's concerned comment). This means that the desired outcome of early intervention (i.e. that all children should be able to start their more formal education with the competence and confidence to allow them to participate fully in school life and achieve their potential) has not been met. If it had, each child would have had their difficulties identified, and a programme of appropriate learning support would have been put in place so that the effects of any difficulties could be reduced. Moreover, all practitioners would be confident and competent in supporting children with a range of special needs conditions. The rhetoric is that this should happen – but sadly, very often the reality falls short of the ideal.

Why should this be? There are many hurdles that may act singly or combine to thwart 'perfect practice.' Some key factors could be:

▶ Practitioners not having had the opportunity or the training to allow them really to understand/observe/analyse the wide range of difficulties children display.
▶ The difficulty of identifying these difficulties and the implications for the children, their teachers and their parents or carers when they appear.

▶ Limited resources, both material (e.g. a climbing frame or outdoor space where the children can play) and human (e.g. not enough staff to make sufficient time-consuming observations, or inexperienced staff who have not worked with children with additional learning needs before).

▶ Conflict with parents who are either over-anxious, not really interested in their children's education in school or in denial that a difficulty exists. Sometimes the parents feel inadequate – 'Was it my fault? Is there a way to be a good parent that I don't know about?' – and they are searching for extended support for themselves as well as their children.

▶ The idea that it is wrong to give children 'a label' showing that they have a learning difficulty too soon.

The process of identifying children who need extra support and communicating this to parents and psychologists also houses many pitfalls, not least because the child at home and the child at nursery and school may present as quite different beings. This may be because the child at home is continuously at the centre of attention, while at nursery this individual contact time must be shared. Or the difference between the ethos of the home and that of the nursery/school context may be confusing, even overwhelming, for some children. Different rules about hitting and retaliating, about sharing toys and social behaviour at table, about listening and attending and dealing with frustration – all of these can be a hidden source of conflict. Children who have been overly sheltered may have to learn to become independent, while those who have had lots of freedom may see being held within the nursery as restricting and inhibiting, especially if they are not particularly interested in what is happening there. Or – and this is a huge or – they may not have the ability or confidence to cope with the skills that are required. When one considers how young they are, the range of competences they need in order to cope with all the activities at nursery is staggering! Some examples are shown in Table 1.2.

Given that there are so many things to look out for, are there priorities for studying children in these early days? At a first or early meeting, nursery staff would probably observe and assess:

▶ any sign of distress or aggression (an emotional competence);
▶ the children's ability to listen and to talk clearly (an intellectual competence);

9

■ TABLE 1.2 Some of the many competences required at nursery

On first arrival	After some months
Talk clearly so as to be understood	Recognise own name and some letters and numbers
Settle in the midst of other children in a large space	Engage in imaginative play
Be prepared for parents/carers to leave for a spell	
Sit and listen to a story	Control a pencil to write and draw
Find a friend	Solve simple problems
Complete a jigsaw	Work with other children
Play alongside then interact with another child	Pay attention: listen and remember
Stay with one activity for a time (concentrate/persevere)	
Be able to take turns	Follow the rules of social interaction
Hold a pencil to write and draw	Be responsible for own bag/books/ lunch box, etc.
Cope with coats and hats	Tie laces and fasten zips/buttons
Enjoy being out of doors	Follow the routine and organisation of the lesson/classroom. Tidy up
Join in pretend games	Catch a ball/ride a bike
Crawl/climb on the climbing frame	

▶ their willingness to stay without becoming distressed (an emotional competence);

▶ ability to move around confidently and handle the resources carefully (a motor or movement competence).

Once these basic competences are achieved, a little later the children's social interaction would be gauged. This would include:

▶ turn-taking as well as willingness to share with the other children;

▶ the ability to play.

Then, as the early-years curriculum unfolds, the competences outlined in the curriculum documents (see Appendix 1) would form a

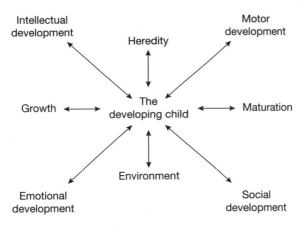

Intellectual development
Motor development
Heredity
Growth
The developing child
Maturation
Environment
Emotional development
Social development

FIGURE 1.1 Different aspects of development

battery of formative assessments. So, the competences for observation have an unwritten but implicit hierarchy.

All these are developmental competences, and while they happen over time, any delay or difference from the norm does affect the children's overall development, for all aspects of development are linked, one affecting the other (Figure 1.1).

Think of the children who cannot climb on the climbing frame, jump off and roll on the mat. This is a wonderful confidence – giving activity for any nursery child – one that boosts their emotional development as well as their movement skills. Those who are afraid to try miss out on the planning and sequencing of movements (motor development) and all the spatial decision-making experiences that are part of the task. 'Not being able to do' means they are left out of friendship groups (social development), and as the activity develops and becomes not simply jumping off but flying to the sky, they are denied the shared planning (intellectual development), which develops both imagination and memory.

One of the hardest decisions early-years staff have to make is whether a child's difficulty is severe enough or long-lasting enough to merit asking for referral to a psychologist for a formal diagnosis. The alternative is to give extra support or a longer time in nursery and hope the child will mature through the difficulties. In school, once children are 6 or 7 and difficulties persist, then requests for referral are accepted, but in the nursery, practitioners are often told that the children are too

11

young for an accurate diagnosis of difficulties to be made – difficulties, that is, of the kind that would warrant a 'label'. This 'wait and see' policy can be very difficult for nursery staff who recognise the importance and timeliness of early specialist support. (NB: different regions have different policies on this. Practitioners have to check what happens where.)

What difficulties would cause concern and what could be done prior to any referral decision? Obviously, very young children need time to settle, but even transitory difficulties should be recorded and dated, ideally on a daily basis as evidence of progress. As useful pointers, consider recording the progress of a child who:

- ▶ can't cope with the nursery's activities;
- ▶ shows inappropriate behaviour, e.g. continual distress, or aggression;
- ▶ refuses to speak, or shouts out inappropriately;
- ▶ doesn't understand what is said;
- ▶ can't follow a story;
- ▶ can't hold eye contact;
- ▶ relies heavily on routine – is upset by change;
- ▶ has ungainly awkward movements (poor balance/co-ordination);
- ▶ can't cross the midline of the body;
- ▶ can't plan ahead – has poor organisation/coping skills;
- ▶ can't be still;
- ▶ is overly protective of personal space;
- ▶ won't share or take turns;
- ▶ can't bear to be touched (but annoys others by touching them);
- ▶ has poor body and spatial awareness (trips and breaks toys).

Having just one or two of those difficulties may indicate traits that in themselves are manageable. It is when several occur together that careful observation and recording over time and in different contexts is a 'must'.

Alternatively, perhaps the decision to seek referral depends on what the key difficulties are and what support is available. After all, is there any point in formal assessment beyond the confines of the school if it does not lead to specialist support? This is an important question, because the very fact of identifying the children who need additional support may change the expectations of parents and practitioners, and this change in expectations in turn can have a negative effect on the growing child. The question is even more fundamental when the parents do not suspect that a problem exists. How soon do they need to know?

The way that message is conveyed is critically important. Kim, an experienced Scottish nursery teacher, tells how she breaks the news. She explains:

> You have to break this kind of news gently. Drip-feed the idea that there could be something wrong. Ask, 'Do you notice that sometimes Adam doesn't seem to understand what he's been asked to do? In nursery, although he does his best to please us, he does what he thinks he should do rather than what he's been asked to do. Yesterday when I said, "Adam, bring your book over to me and I'll read a story with you", he ran and put his book on the library shelf — that's what he does to help at tidy up time. Could you look out for things like that at home?'
>
> Then, if the difficulty persists, I'd say, 'I would like [the psychologist] to meet Adam. I think she might be able to suggest some ways to give extra ideas to help this. There may be nothing wrong, but as the waiting lists are long, I feel we should put his name down now. Would you think that was a good idea?'

(In regions where special educational needs co-ordinators (SENCOs) are involved, they should be involved in all discussions and in contacting parents rather than teachers communicating with parents directly.)

Another debate arises if the child has a difficulty confirmed. What then? Should the other children be told? This of course would depend on the parents' wishes — and no school would transgress those — but many older children with a 'hidden handicap' are frustrated because no one recognises their difficulty. As a result, they land up being not the same as the other children but with a different 'label' — one that says they are lazy, stupid or badly behaved. Surely that is much worse? Children don't tease children with Down's syndrome because they are helped to understand that these children need a bit of extra support. Should we be more up-front? If not, are we denying that differences exist? But of course no one can foretell what the future holds for any child. Although many special needs conditions do not go away, much can be done to assist so that the label does not stick. Just another point to ponder!

There are different theories about the cause of these difficulties, and researchers are gathering evidence to verify or refute them. Some of the hypotheses concern:

► changes in lifestyle, e.g. a more confined but rushed lifestyle denying the children practice in what previously were considered basic skills, such as sitting at table using a knife and fork; free play outdoors promoting independence and decision-making;

► a genetic influence where difficulties are passed on through the generations, such as difficulty with reading and spelling; clumsiness; autism;

► nutritional differences, such as the explosion of additives in children's food; over-reliance on fatty or sugary foods; gluten intolerance;

► neurological differences, such as different arrangements of cells in the brain: slower myelination of the axons (the spindles leading from the neurones and carrying the 'instructions') from the sensory input;

► hormonal differences, such as too much testosterone in the developing fetus or lack of dopamine at the synapses between the brain cells (neurones);

► physical differences, such as a smaller corpus callosum in boys; obese children not willing or not able to exercise; poor muscle tone (hypotonia); hyperflexibility.

Research into factors affecting children and treatments to help them is fraught with difficulties. How can any researcher be sure what parents and children on a research programme explicitly do? If children find it difficult to swallow and the research programme into the efficacy of nutritional supplements requires that they take capsules each day, is it not likely that some of the children involved will refuse to comply? Moral questions too must be considered – for example, if a new 'treatment' is thought to be beneficial, how ethical is it to withhold it from one group for the sake of comparing its effects? And when can researchers be sure that any side effects can be controlled? The current debates over the effects of the MMR immunisation and of prescribing medication to calm children illustrate the dilemmas.

This chapter has outlined some of the issues that concern early-years practitioners as they suspect that some of the children in their care are not coping as well as they should for their age, in view of their circumstances and the amount of support they have received. These will be raised again as the subsequent chapters provide information about:

▶ different additional learning needs;
▶ ways to observe the children with a view to gathering objective evidence of their difficulties in a range of contexts; and
▶ strategies that have been shown to help.

From the points outlined in this chapter, it can be seen that the task of making accurate observations and assessments is fraught with difficulties. One strategy that has not been tried and that might provide a rich source of 'evidence' is to say to the children themselves, to 'Tell me, what could we do to make things better?' Then, of course, adults need to listen carefully to what they have to say. Many children who have the difficulties mentioned are highly intelligent and are able to reflect and tell. Their perceptions about their time in nursery may have been underestimated. Perhaps they may reveal things adults do not know? This hypothesis will be tested in this book, which is all about listening to children who are experiencing difficulties, and listening to their parents and to their teachers so that strategies to help can be realistic and 'shareable' with many other children who need support.

Chapter 2

Listen to the children explain their difficulties

In the following case studies, children offer their ideas on what is preventing them enjoying and making the most of their learning at nursery. The children's comments are followed by strategies for support that resulted from the information that was gleaned from the children.

MARK

 Listen to Mark, who is nearly 4:

> Yes, I go to nursery every day and nights too because it's dark outside sometimes. It's good at snack [time] but I don't like stories about dogs and things. I want to go to the park because you can run around there – run and run and not stop at all.

Mark's nursery nurse, Fiona, was very alarmed by his hyperactivity:

> He won't wait, he won't listen to me at all. He just runs off. He's very nimble and I make sure I take him into the nursery yard whenever I can because I want him to get rid of his pent-up energy, but he tries to jump over the fence and I know I couldn't jump it, so I'm frightened he'll run off. He's like a caged lion, he really is.

His mother, Anne, gave her side of things:

> As soon as I could, I got him a place at this nursery because it has a big yard and bikes to keep him occupied. I was desperate for a break, as he has me at screaming pitch. He jumps down stairs without looking and dashes into the road. I just can't cope. The health visitor

thought he'd improve once his tablets [a fish oil supplement] worked and the teachers got hold of him, but they can't control him either. He's not cheeky and he doesn't hurt the other children, but he is wild. He has to run till *everyone* is exhausted. I asked my doctor if he had ADHD but he said he was far too young to diagnose that, otherwise I'd have told the nursery.

(See also Chapter 10.)

Anne and the nursery practitioners set up a plan:

▶ Mark's mum would take him to the park each morning for a good run around so that he had the best chance of settling down for a spell.

▶ Fiona would watch him carefully and praise him for being still for a moment or two. This was a positive behaviour strategy: 'Catch him being good'.

▶ She would anticipate his frustration, and when he became restless she would invite him to go outside so that he would think he was 'following instructions' rather than losing control and defying the staff. (An auxiliary was appointed to give extra cover in the nursery.)

▶ He would have milk for breakfast rather than juice, and on the paediatrician's advice he would continue to take a fish oil supplement each day.

The nursery teacher then gave her reflections:

It's been hard, but that's what inclusion is all about. Mark is a nice boy, but it took us four weeks to get through to him. Once he started charging around, some of the others thought they would join in too, so we had to rearrange the furniture so that there were no straight spaces for them to run through. Luckily, the others were more interested in the activities and the stories, but it could have gone the other way. And of course you're not supposed to restrain children, but we had to. We were afraid he'd go through the windows!

After four horrendous weeks he did settle, and the combination of the diet change and the routine and the positive behaviour input has helped. He likes woodwork and spends a lot of time hammering bits of wood together. I *think* he is settling down.

17

JACK

 Now listen to Jack, who is 4.

Jack is in his first term at nursery and already he is finding life difficult. He tells his tale.

> Mum, what is valuable time? That lady is always saying I'm wasting it, but I don't know what I did that was bad. Am I a bad boy? Is that why the other boys won't let me play? Can I stay at home with you now? I've been lots of years at nursery and I hate it. It's always too noisy with boys stomping around and it's far too bright and it smells so bad as well. Why don't they turn all the lights off because they hurt my eyes and they go all watery – and that horrible girl Julie told everyone I was a cry-baby and I'm not.

(See also Chapter 7.)

Action 1: Parents

Jack's parents immediately contacted the nursery to relay his comments about the strong lights. In response, Jack's teacher, Marie, explained:

> I was really surprised to hear this, because for most of the day the children are free to move around the nursery and they can mostly choose where to go to do their work. Naturally I was glad to be told, for I had never heard of a child with this difficulty. I assured Jack's parents that I would check where he sat when he was at the writing table or at snack. This would make sure that he wasn't facing the large windows and that he was not directly under any strong light. I'll also make sure I switch off the nursery lights [they were the long tubular type and occasionally flickered] when I can.
>
> I knew Jack's parents had arranged [for Jack] to see the optician, so I asked them to come into class after that to discuss things. I knew about Jack's asthma and allergies, so I was doubly anxious not to cause the child any unnecessary trauma.

Action 2: Parents

At first, Jack's parents were reluctant to mention the 'smells problem', fearing it might cause offence. However, they had read up about sensory hypersensitivity and knew from Jack's reaction that he was distressed by strong smells. The invitation to come into nursery for an extended meeting with Jack present had reassured them that the teacher was genuinely interested and willing to do all she could to ease Jack's day, so the subject of bad smells was raised!

Marie was bemused by the 'smells' problem. She was at a loss, as the nursery building was fairly new. However, Jack was able to explain that the air freshener (which the teacher had provided to illustrate a lesson on the different senses) and the scented soap, which she had provided in the toilets for the same reason, had 'made his nose sting and his eyes water'. She also realised that the 'wet pants' issue might be down to Jack avoiding the toilets, which had been disinfected. Any timing change (i.e. discussing the possibility of cleaning the nursery toilets first so that the smell had time to diffuse before the children arrived, and possibly using a different antiseptic) needed co-operation from the cleaning staff. They were delighted to be consulted, considering this an environmental issue that directly affected the children.

Other points from Jack's original self-evaluation

From further reflections on Jack's comments, it became apparent that planning and organising himself and his resources was a difficulty, so Jack was monitored closely to observe signs of specific learning difficulties. In effect, as his confidence grew (which it did once the offending lights and smells were removed), his organisational skills improved too. Perhaps removing the distracters had allowed him to concentrate on what he was trying to do?

Jack also felt he was being left out of games, so the nursery nurses carried out unobtrusive observations in the playground. They wanted to find whether 'not getting to play' was a regular occurrence or whether Jack was smarting with hurt from just one incident. They considered this to be an important distinction, because adults can make situations worse by intervening just when the child is finding ways to cope. In effect they found that Jack was hanging back, finding it difficult to get into an outdoor game rather than being consciously left out. To try to counteract this, they suggested a ball game and gave Jack the ball to start it off. He was in!

Marie's comment

Jack is obviously sensitive and willing to share his worries, so there shouldn't be any delay in finding out the extent of his difficulties and putting strategies to help in place. We shall do all we can to boost his confidence. We think he needs time to mature but we have plenty of it. He will be all right.

Parents' reflection

After Jack was encouraged to work in a quieter, less bright spot, he immediately reported, 'I can see things better now', and he appeared to be a much happier child. Now that she was more aware of his social difficulties, the teacher allowed him and one or two other reluctant children to stay inside to play for a week or two. She explained that this would happen 'till the weather improves because the wet could affect Jack's asthma', but really it was to give her time to build his confidence and prevent him having to face up to the bustle outside.

Headteacher's comment

The support staff in school have really blossomed by being involved in real learning issues instead of always – as they told me – being 'on the fringe of anything important with no one really taking notice of what we say'. I hadn't realised they would want to be involved like this, but after I had checked confidentiality issues, I invited them to take part in a whole-staff discussion on 'environmental factors affecting the children'. I think we are a more coherent school now. Anyway, the inspectors were pleased. They wanted us to keep a diary about 'our innovation' (their words) and promised they would ask for evaluations later in the year.

This accolade had been an unexpected bonus for the school. As a result, the headteacher was anxious to see 'inclusion' work for all staff as well as pupils.

Key points

▶ Practitioners should check for environmental 'hazards', such as bright lights and strong smells, and monitor children who rub their eyes or show sensory distress. The children may not realise that their difficulty is not shared by others and not take time to explain.

▶ Removing unnecessary stress factors can allow children to concentrate on learning.

▶ Including playground and support staff in discussions about how to support the children can reinforce the inclusive ethos of a school, although issues of confidentiality have to be addressed.

JULIE

Now consider 4-year-old Julie, the child who was unkind to Jack. Julie resolutely refused to respond to Marie (the teacher)'s question 'Would you like to tell me what kinds of things you like to do best?'. She would not hold eye contact and her rigid posture signalled distress and resentment.

Action 1: Marie (teacher) and Dave (nursery nurse)

As a result of their informal observations, the adults decided to monitor how Julie was interacting with the other children by using a time-sampling method of data gathering (Table 2.1). Both Marie and Dave had been concerned that she was not settling down and was showing early signs of antagonism and isolation. She sometimes followed Jack around but didn't really have a friend. Was this a significant finding raising questions of possible Asperger's syndrome or was it a sign of some transient unhappiness or a speech and language difficulty?

Action 2: Teacher

Marie's first intervention was to have the two children (Jack and Julie) work together on building a collage for the wall from cut-out hand-prints all the children had produced. Having observed that they both selected painting or drawing at choosing time, she explained that they had been chosen as 'art stars'. This seemed to be working until Julie shouted out that Jack had put pieces on upside down – he had – and Jack burst into tears. When Julie asserted she 'didn't want to do it anyway' and stomped off laughing, the staff were concerned that she had not developed altruism (understanding how her actions impacted on the feelings of others). They had noticed her spoiling other children's

■ TABLE 2.1 Time sampling (to gather evidence about the quality of children's interacting. Child's name: Julie; observer: Anna; date: 6 May 2004

Time	Observation
10.02	Julie stands by the radiator, humming. Alex approaches, then stops, waits (beckoning her to join in his game), then he runs off. Julie pays no attention; doesn't attempt to follow him. She deliberately avoids catching his eye.
10.04	Julie runs to fetch a red bus, comes back to the radiator and bangs it on the metal, making a loud din. Freya hides her ears and shouts, 'Stop that noise'. Julie doesn't respond. She does start to yell out accompanying the bangs, 'Yeh, yeh, yeh'.
10.05	I try to divert Julie by offering to paint with her. She leaves the radiator and appears to be joining me but then runs over to the outside door and announces, 'Boys need to go out to climb trees'. NB. Note strange response – ? Does she know she's a girl?
10.06	It's very cold, but Julie won't have her coat on – she runs out and races to the top of the climbing frame still carrying the red bus. She is very agile, with no fear of heights.
10.08	I say, 'I'm shivering, please come inside'. Julie pays no attention. She is not rude, just uninterested as if I wasn't there.
10.10	Suddenly she rushes down and gathers up leaves. Other children come out but Julie ignores them. She goes back indoors. She is smiling to herself but appears unaware of her surroundings.

games and throwing their coats on the floor, and this was another example of unacceptable behaviour.

Julie shrugged off any offers of support. She was only prepared to do her own thing, which was disconcerting to say the least.

Julie's mother, Jacquie, was unwilling to come into school, so a home visit was arranged. She explained that she had no idea how to cope with Julie's tantrums and that she was at her wits' end. She had hoped that going to school would resolve the problem. Jacquie admitted that Julie had not settled at her first nursery, so 'I just took her away and that saved us having to get there in the mornings'. She explained that Julie didn't go to bed until she did, because the noise in the flats frightened her and so 'neither of us can get up in time. We had an alarm once but it got broken so we don't have anything except the tele now – but you have to waken up to put that on, so it's no use'.

Action 3: Teacher

Marie used puppets and made up a story about the poor mole that wouldn't come out of the ground because no one was kind. The children handled the puppets and discussed what they would do to make Mole happier – that is, encourage him to play and wait until he was ready. Through that role-play she hoped the children would see how their actions could affect another person.

Generally the staff had found that interacting with Julie was unrewarding, for 'she looked straight through us'. Different nursery nurses were assigned to see if they could make a breakthrough by finding her interests and building a relationship. Careful daily recording was done to show the line manager in case referral to a psychologist was required at a later date.

SIMON

Now listen to 4-year-old Simon. Simon is full of fun. He was brimming with enthusiasm at the start of nursery, but now in his second session he is becoming frustrated by his poor motor skills. He explains:

> I want to ride the bike but I can only do the trike. That's for the wee ones. An' threading an' stuff. That's hard because the thing won't go through the hole but Jack's does. At snack it's OK if it's apple or celery but not toast because it gets all churned up with the butter. I fell off the climbing frame another day and that was sore. I want to climb up and jump off but I'm doing it tomorrow.

Sarah, his mother, describes life at home with Simon:

> He is just so untidy, but that's boys for you – and he's a bit lazy – boys again. He waits for me to dress him, would you believe. I know we do too much for him, but he's such a great kid, he really is. He does things like bringing me juice in the morning. Usually he spills some, but the important thing is that he does it.
>
> We sometimes laugh at him because his yoghurt goes all over his face rather than in his mouth, and no, he can't catch a ball yet, but his Dad and me, we never were any use at sports either. He's so

bright at reading and can spell words so we just thought, well, he couldn't be good at everything and we are glad he has the abilities he does have.

Kevin, his nursery teacher, explains why he is concerned:

> I first noticed that Simon had difficulty holding a pencil, although he could manage one of the thick paintbrushes. But he changed hands all the time and when I asked him he said it was because his hands were too tired. When we sang 'Incy Wincy Spider' with actions, Simon wasn't able to join in. His hands were rather floppy, so we began to concentrate on strengthening exercises. We are lucky to have an occupational therapist coming into our primary school and she was able to give us some advice.

Kevin had helped the PE teacher in school to set up an early-years movement programme for reception/Primary 1 children and she assured us that Simon's name would be added to her list. In the meantime, Simon practised finger-strengthening exercises, and his mum was anxious to join in once she realised that he could be held back by poor motor skills, even although he was an intelligent boy. (See Chapter 6.)

LEAH

Leah is 3. She won't talk at all, so Cat, her nursery nurse, explains her concerns:

> Leah is a very quiet child; in fact, she chooses not to speak at all in nursery, although her Mum says she chats at home. She always looks so anxious to please. Very often some of the more confident children tell her what to do – and she does it, or they just leave her in peace. She doesn't seem to mind either way. I thought that if I played alongside her she would open up and speak, but the most I ever get is a smile. How are we to assess her language development? She doesn't seem unhappy, so what's wrong?

Leah may be feeling insecure and prefer not to talk in new situations or with people she doesn't know. She may just need time. This is selective mutism, which comes under the heading of speech and language impairments. Cat should continue to build her confidence through spending time with her and trying to read her body language so that she can respond appropriately even within the silence. Once a relationship is established, Cat can pretend to misunderstand – for example, when Leah wants a piece of fruit at snack time, she could offer her a biscuit and hope she'll be tempted to say 'no' and go on to say what she does want!

The fact that she speaks at home is an indication that all will be well. Leah's parents could be asked to tape some of the things she says to let the staff hear her speech and possibly to indicate any special interests that might prompt speech in the nursery. They should also be asked if they can always understand what Leah says, whether she willingly speaks to strangers and whether *they* can understand her. This is important, because home people can have their ears attuned and not recognise that there is a speech difficulty. (See Chapter 5.)

COLIN

Colin is nearly 4 and talks a great deal to anyone who is around, whether they listen or not. Niamh, his nursery teacher, tells her tale:

> When Colin came into nursery, he told us all about coming on the number 32 bus and every detail of the bus – the size, the diesel engine, the colour, its route. We were very impressed by his knowledge although we realised that his talk was going on and on. We thought that was just him being nervous. He was clutching his bus ticket, and when I tried to take it from him he flared up and grabbed it back. I didn't think too much about it at the time.
>
> But the next day he told me the same detailed story all over again and I noticed that he was looking past me over my shoulder. He seemed a lovable little boy, always wanting to hug me. He wouldn't play with the other children at all; only make his toy bus make roads in the sand or travel over piles of blocks in the construction corner. He also seemed very tense. At singing time we chose 'The Wheels on the Bus' to see if he would join in, but he wasn't interested. I think it was too babyish for him.
>
> When the health visitor came to nursery, we asked her to observe Colin. She was very concerned that Colin was demonstrating signs of Asperger's syndrome. She explained that when he ran for a hug,

he wasn't being loving, as I'd thought, but pushing my face aside to avoid any eye contact. That was a blow, I can tell you.

(See Chapter 10 for more on Asperger's syndrome.)

Strategies to support Colin

The health visitor advised Niamh:

- ▶ to begin where Colin's interest lay – that is, in buses;
- ▶ to see if he would listen if Niamh told him about her own journey on the bus;
- ▶ to set out a bus route and explain, for example, that the bus went past the bus station or the hospital, and thereby gradually extend the possibilities for talk;
- ▶ to have a pass-the-parcel type game in a very small group to involve him in the beginnings of sharing through giving and receiving.

The practitioners were also advised that the nursery environment might be too colourful and busy, and that Colin could be overwhelmed by the patterns and the movements of mobiles the children had made. The nursery staff organised a 'chill-out corner' that was quiet and calming. The coloured cushions were replaced by beige-covered ones, and room dividers were rearranged to give a private space. A tape recorder with sounds and music was left there so that any child could control their environment by only having the music if they found it soothing.

After six months, Niamh said that Colin had made some progress in that he would stay longer listening to a story. She thought the quiet corner had been very beneficial in giving him the quiet he needed.

Colin's parents were not anxious to give any details of how they found his speech at home. They explained that they had considered his chatter advanced for his age even though it was mainly limited to buses. They were concerned at his 'looking away' but thought he was a very warm little boy, giving cuddles all the time. Also, he was a good boy, giving no trouble in a household of four other boys who were noisy all the time.

SAM

Now listen to Sam's nursery teacher, Tim:

Sam is a child who can't explain how he feels. He had epilepsy as a baby and his dad blames that for his developmental delay. Sam is not toilet trained and has difficulty standing unsupported for any length of time. He is a third child and Dad Jay, (now a single parent with responsibility for the children) told me why he was insisting that Sam go to mainstream nursery and, later, mainstream school. He was sure that was the right thing for the family. Jay explained, 'When you have a child who has a disability, life for all the family changes – not just for the parents. I think it's different if it's a first child, because then there's only that child to consider. But I have three boys, and because we have to spend our lives thinking about what will be best for Sam, it's tough for the others. So after the first huge disappointment of realising Sam was going to need a huge amount of support, we decided to make life as normal as possible so that our other two didn't suffer and begin to resent him. By the time Sam was 3 he was over his fits, so I took him to nursery to let him mix with children his own age. Well, he didn't mix, but he wasn't unhappy, and it gave me a breathing space to get things done. When the other two came home, they could ask him how he got on. This gave us a little bit of normality. He couldn't say much, of course, but he wanted to be asked and looked as if he remembered, and so there was real communication – he was making a little progress and we feel he will speak more soon.

When he was 4 and the question of "what school" came up, we decided to take the choice of mainstream for Sam. From a practical point of view, that school was just along the road and his brothers could take him. There was also the question of cost. Having a child with very special needs is expensive, because so much gets spilled on or broken. On bad days he needs three sets of clothes, and with the other two at school I have to buy the uniforms and the school-bags and all the kit. The school have a language unit and he will get a special needs auxiliary. We know the teachers and they know me and that's important too. If they have to phone and say, "Come and get Sam," I know he's unhappy, but I know he's safe and they haven't delayed too long wondering how I'll react.

The main thing is that when Sam goes to this school I'll get a break, and if things work out, I'll be able to do some part-time work. That would help out and make us feel a bit more normal.'

Listen to nursery teacher Liz's response after two terms with Sam. She explains:

I was quite apprehensive about having Sam. Although I didn't expect him to fit, he did make strange noises. I wondered how the other children would react. It's strange, because they don't seem to notice. They do realise Sam's different, but they just accept him. We didn't explain anything to them. They are just 3 and 4 after all, so it's been interesting to see how they take everything in their stride. Sam has Diane, his special needs auxiliary, with him all day, and after a short time in the group, she takes him away to do his own work. Sam can't cope with the usual nursery curriculum yet, although he is recognising his own name and seems to enjoy stories. They have to be short, and if they have big, simple pictures, he can point out the dog's tail, things like that, so we can see he's making some progress. Whenever he gets distressed and shouts too much or flaps his arms, Diane takes him out into the parents' room. We keep that dark so that Sam can have a sleep if he wants. I couldn't manage without her, but that's not real inclusion, is it?

Asked if the other parents had made any comments, she replied:

Not yet. I keep waiting, but no one has mentioned Sam at all. Of course, it's a small group and the family are well known in the area, so that will help. Sam's not aggressive to the other children, so he can sit with them for a whole story on good days. He watches the other children and is trying to do what they do. That's progress. I don't know what will happen when he's older, though.

GILLY

Now listen to Gilly. Gilly is a 6-year-old who has Down's syndrome. She had spent an extra year in nursery and had been happy there. As Gilly's IQ was low, the family was given the choice of sending her to a special school, but both Gilly and her parents wished her to attend the local primary school. Gilly explains why:

I want to be with Sarah and go to her school. She is my best friend.
I don't want to go in the taxi every day, for it's quite a long way and we
don't get rounders and I can nearly hit the ball now and it's good fun.
I have to work hard but I'm getting new socks and a blue jersey and
Sarah will look after me at playtime. It's good.

Gilly's parents explain some more of the reasoning behind the decision:

We were very pleased to hear about the chance of Gilly attending
mainstream school because education is surely more than being able
to do school subjects, is it not? Gilly loves to play with Sarah and
her friends, and was very unhappy at the thought of going off to a
different school each day. She wondered why, and it was hard to
explain. One day she asked if it was because she was stupid, and we
were so upset, for no one had ever mentioned that. We did visit the
special school, and the staff were lovely and really interested in Gilly,
but we couldn't see her making much progress there. She does tend
to just go with the flow and will be quite happy daydreaming!
We thought that she would cause no trouble but not push herself
to learn, either. Happiness was the first concern of the school, and,
while this is so understandable, we hoped that there would be a
higher set of expectations for her in the mainstream school.

The other children at the special school were more severely
disabled. The other child with Down's syndrome had no language at
all, and after the preliminary visit, Gilly was beginning to copy his
signing, which worried us. Some of the children needed feeding,
some were just learning to walk, most didn't converse, and the staff
were naturally spending a great deal of time supporting them. But
Gilly could do all these things.

We've tried not to smother her [so as] to make her as independent as possible. Another worry was that when she would get home
in the afternoon, she would have no school friends who live locally.
Sarah lives nearby, but naturally she would want to talk about her
own school, and if Gilly didn't go there, she wouldn't understand
the people or the routine. We could see the friendship wavering. And
so we made an application for Gilly to go to mainstream school. We
just pray we've done the right thing.

Before deciding, we went to the primary school and tried to see
it though Gilly's eyes. She was so keen to go there we had to agree,
but we had lots of qualms. Would the children make fun of Gilly

because she was quite slow to learn new things and would have to have different books? Would she come to *believe* she was stupid? She was used to playing with a very small group of children who knew her. Would she cope with the larger numbers, and, without a grown-up at her side all the time, would she remember what she had to do? We went to the school to see if the staff there could help.

Gilly's new teacher, Eva, met Gilly's parents to explain what she anticipated would happen. She drew a positive picture:

I have a lovely class of children and I had no fears that Gilly would not be made welcome. In fact, it's the opposite. They want to do everything for her – they want to take her hand and sharpen her pencil and find her books. The downside is that Gilly just smiles and is happy to let them. Once she has settled down I'll need to put a stop to that, for she will soon become deskilled.

When Moira, the headteacher, asked me, or rather told me, about Gilly coming, I was concerned because I already had children with a wide range of ability in the class and I have to differentiate work to suit all the levels. Also, I didn't know much about Down's syndrome, so I wasn't sure how to cope. And although the children in this class wouldn't tease her, there are youngsters in other classes who might pick on Gilly just because she's small for her age and looks a bit different. I wondered if my children would be able to protect her, or even if it was fair to ask them.

The joy was that I was able to have a special needs assistant for part of each day. She took over some of the administration and spent time overseeing the top group till I worked out what Gilly knew and how quickly she could learn. She stays with my class for all the practical work, but goes to the resource teacher at maths time. She has an Early Intervention programme for maths. That works at the minute because we have setting in this school and the children do move around, but I don't know how it will work later on. Certainly we don't want Gilly going out of class to be taught on her own, for that's exclusion – not what she's here for. She's no trouble in class and she loves to be here. The difficulty is in keeping her focused, because she's so easily distracted. She uses her social skills – smiling and hugging – to get out of tackling her work. That's frustrating, but it's hard to resist!

Three months later, Gilly tells about her experiences:

I go to Sarah's school now and it's funny because there's no one that's just like me. I miss Darren [the boy with Down's syndrome at the special school] and I don't think I'm the cleverest any more. Sometimes Sarah doesn't let me play, and that makes me sad. She says they need good runners. I still get to paint lovely pictures and my teacher is very pleased with me. She's giving me real sums and I have my own special reading book. That's cool!

Eva gives her account:

Having Gilly is a huge responsibility. She's a delightful, smiling child for much of the day, but I worry that I'm not doing enough for her. She really needs more time than I can give her, because my lowest-achieving group is still too far ahead to share much of the work. So Gilly is really another group on her own! I have to prepare special teaching plans and individual worksheets at night along with every-thing else, and then in class it takes time to explain what's needed. My assistant is too willing to be diverted by a hug!

The other children have accepted Gilly wholeheartedly, but she has to learn to be more independent now. I can see time-wasting going on in the class, and this didn't happen before. Sometimes they use Gilly as an excuse to get off their own work. Partly because of having Gilly, I have focused on personal and social development themes for the class this year. There is no doubt that the other chil-dren have learned a lot from watching Gilly and looking out for her, and they have been more tolerant of each other. Perhaps they will become more caring people? Unfortunately for Gilly, I have another child with Asperger's syndrome and Tourette's syndrome newly arrived in this class, and he asks questions in a loud voice. These can be hurtful, and I have tried to explain to Gilly that he doesn't mean to be rude, but we often have tears. It seems that the management thought two children with learning difficulties might be friends and that the same work would do for both. It shows how much they understand about the different conditions! Now I am beginning to resent all the extra work.

The headteacher, Moira, reflects:

> I did wonder about having the two children in the same class, but the other one with children of that age group has a probationer teacher, so placing Tim there was not a possibility. Also, it seemed that Gilly had settled so well. I was between a rock and a hard place. The boy with Asperger's and Tourette's should also be able to share Gilly's special needs auxiliary. I was afraid that the school would lose her if she only had one child who was physically well to look after. Eva is a very capable teacher with six or seven years of experience and I am listening to her requests for support and will arrange for her to have time out of the class on a regular basis to do planning or attend CPD [continuing professional development] afternoons. It's on the cards that other children with very special needs will be arriving in school soon, and naturally we shall aim to do our best for them all. The class numbers will be kept steady too. Other new children will have to go into the probationer's class. Life in school is fraught with management problems as well as educational ones. Sometimes I wonder who recognises that.

And so there were plans afoot to support the teacher by giving her time out and some training to help her understand the different conditions. Eva considers that teachers need much more prior warning of children arriving so that they can at least do some reading and prepare to go on courses before the children arrive.

Eva again:

> The biggest problem is the parents – Gilly's parents (who in my view have unrealistic expectations of what she is capable of) and those of the other children. If they would just let me get on with my work, but no. They either want their children to be in a group with Tim and Gilly or they resent them being there. Of course they don't come right out and say that. They have all sorts of ulterior notions, e.g. 'Why has my child not moved on to the next book? His friend in the other class is ahead now.' One parent asked why '*these children*' had come to a 'normal' school. I tried to explain the benefits, but they weren't going to listen, and I know they've been to visit the private school, so we may lose that child and his sister in P4. Maybe I'll get the blame? Life is challenging, is it not?

In this school, the complexity of inclusion was beginning to bite. The staff were anxious to cope, but felt unprepared and under-resourced in terms of reading materials and support strategies. At the same time, they were glad to have the opportunity of working with Gilly and Tim, so there was a definite upside to the innovation.

Eva wondered what else could be done to make inclusion happen. At the moment, Tim was relating well to his auxiliary, and the language unit was providing ideas and resources, so the class teacher's workload was not hugely increased. But was this really inclusion? The answer from the staff was, 'It's as much as it can be.'

To try to answer questions like this, Moira had a staff meeting to explain what inclusion should involve. She explained to the staff that 'inclusion' didn't mean that each child in the class was doing the same thing. Some children already had differentiated work and some went out of the class to do movement programmes or to have extension work, so she asked the teachers to see disabled children as just other children who needed some special provision.

The staff then asked Moira to tell what would happen to children who could not access the curriculum. They were afraid of being thought anti-inclusion, but 'could not stay quiet when they anticipated that children who were significantly disabled would not have the best chance in a mainstream school'. They feared that 'political correctness would mean that children were shoehorned into mainstream', and that 'chemical crutches' such as Ritalin would be used to make the children behave. These were hugely important issues that had not been debated. They had read that inclusive schools were having to consider their first exclusion order (Garner and Gains 2000) and that staff, forced to cope, were leaving the profession. 'Who are the winners?', they asked.

Chapter 3

Communication between parents and practitioners about children with special needs

MAKING INCLUSION WORK

A new headteacher, Jon, tells of his resolve. He explains:

> When I came to this school last year, my ambition was to make inclusion work, and for me that meant I had to convince the staff that including parents to a much greater extent than had previously been the case had to be part of the change. I knew there might be some resistance to the idea. There had been a great deal of scepticism when this was suggested at my old school, but from hearing about positive outcomes from staff communicating with parents and setting up meetings to share observations and assessments, I was eager to give it my best shot. I thought that the first step was to contact the nursery, because they were the group whose main focus was on observing children. The second was to share a letter from a parent to let all the staff share a little of what it must be like to have a child with a disability.

'A trip to Holland': a letter from a parent with a child with a disability

> I am often asked to describe the experience of raising a child with a disability – to try to help people who have not shared that unique experience to understand it, to imagine how it would feel. It's like this.

When you are going to have a baby, it's like planning a fabulous trip to Italy. You buy a bunch of guidebooks and make wonderful plans to see the Colosseum, Michelangelo's David and the gondolas in Venice. You learn some handy phrases in Italian. It's all very exciting!

After months of eager anticipation, the day finally arrives. You pack your bags and off you go. Several hours later, the plane lands. The stewardess comes in and says, 'Welcome to Holland.' 'Holland?', you say. 'What do you mean, Holland? I signed up for Italy. I'm supposed to be in Italy. All my life I've dreamed of going to Italy.'

But there's been a change in the flight plan. You've landed in Holland and there you must stay.' The important thing is that they haven't taken you to a horrible, filthy place, full of famine and disease. It's just a different place, so you must buy new guidebooks and you must learn a whole new language. You will also meet a new group of people you would never have met. It's slower paced than Italy, less flashy than Italy, but after you've been there for a while, you look around and you begin to notice that Holland has windmills, Holland has tulips, Holland even has Rembrandts.

But everyone you know is busy coming and going from Italy, and they are all bragging about what a wonderful time they had there. For the rest of your life you will say, 'Yes, that's where I was supposed to go. That's what I had planned'.

The pain of that will never go away, because the loss of a dream is a very significant loss. But if you spend your life mourning the fact that you didn't get to Italy you may never be free to enjoy the very special, the very lovely things about Holland.

(Written by a mother and an advocate for children with ADD.)

The headteacher continued:

I used this letter as a stimulus for discussion at a CPD meeting with a group of local schools. One or two of the less experienced teachers said that although they sympathised, the letter didn't give them any hints on how to communicate, while others commented that they felt quite humbled and that they wanted to find out more about how parents coped with the children full-time at home. A further finding was that some staff said they hadn't thought about the parents' struggles and disappointments much before and they had now begun to recognise how difficult life could be. They assured me that they would listen to parents with a new-found sympathy. They also wanted to be reassured that 'management' would allocate time for discussions with parents, beginning with nursery practitioners, who were expecting children with more complex needs than had been in their classes before.

The time issue was the nub of the subsequent discussion, and ways of contacting parents and welcoming them into nursery or school were listed. The first ones were:

▶ letters of introduction before the children arrived in nursery or school;

▶ letters asking the parents whether and how they would like to be involved in school life;

▶ invitations to arrange individual and lengthier meetings for parents of children with special needs rather than the 'usual churn-around where everyone lands up exhausted' (teacher's reflection on usual parents' evenings).

Introductory letters were already part of the welcoming arrangements, but the staff decided to try to merge the first two ideas to save the parents feeling bombarded with paper. The learning support staff agreed to discuss ways of initiating the third idea and assured nursery staff that their views would be taken on board. As a result, the head 'had a feeling they were coming onside, even although many of them were reluctant to volunteer to try to write the letters'.

Those who did shared the draft shown on pp. 38–9.

Organisation

The next issue to be discussed was organisation:

? Who was to be responsible for collating the replies and sorting out when the parents were to come into nursery or school?

? What security measures were to be put in place? What about disclosure issues?

? Could parents come into school at times other than the pre-arranged ones if they so wished?

? What spaces were to be allocated for a parents' room, and was keeping them out of the nursery staffroom fostering inclusion? Would special needs teachers not resent giving up their teaching space for the parents if their room was hardly used?

? Who was to set the parameters of what the parents were to do, and how was this different from the duties of the nursery nurses, who were trained and paid for the job? Who would explain the difference to the parents?

? How would some children feel if their parents could not or would not come?

? Who was to persuade parents to leave if this became necessary?

Sadly, time or other constraints such as those listed often prevent the important people in the children's lives – the children themselves, their parents and teachers – getting together for long enough for each to understand the perspective of the other. Such understanding is vital if they are to appreciate the difficulties that beset the children and discover what positive strategies work best at home and at school. Without this communication, valuable time can be lost and much energy wasted in reinventing the wheel or trying out things that do not work. This would seem to be common sense. Yet even when meetings between parents and teachers do happen, there can be communication difficulties that prevent a frank and open sharing of what is amiss and what the best ways forward might be. Most teachers nowadays are anxious to meet parents so that they can work together to help the children. That is the rhetoric. The reality, however, is that both parties can feel inadequate, not sure of the role they have to play, and be left wondering about how the other is assessing them.

Woolfendale (1992) must have shared these reflections when she wrote:

The premise behind consultation with parents is that it is a good idea to ask parents what they think about the school their children attend. While this is beautifully simple as a premise, translation into reality, with no historical precedent of course, takes considerable hard work and commitment.

It must be much more difficult when children have special needs.

Hornton Nursery Class
Tel. 0100 21345
29 April 2004

Dear _____,

The staff at Hornton Nursery would like to invite all parents/carers to a first individual meeting to get to know one another. The purpose of the meeting is to find the best ways of working together to support your children. Each meeting will last for twenty minutes or so and the discussion will be entirely confidential. No other parent or child will know what was discussed. A cup of tea or coffee will be available and some of our senior pupils will look after any younger children in the nursery if this eases childcare problems. Older brothers and sisters who attend this school may stay in their own classroom.

As organising a large number of meetings needs careful organisation, please send the tear-off part of this letter back to school by Wednesday 3rd May. If you accept, a further letter will then be sent to you suggesting times and places. We would be glad if you could keep to these times or notify us of unexpected change as soon as possible. The order of invitations being sent out has no significance; all parents will be invited to come in at various times during the term. The teachers and support staff look forward to the meetings.

Please be ready with questions or suggestions and/or raise any issue that concerns you.

Thank you for completing this invitation. We hope that this kind of collaboration will smooth your child's entry into nursery and his/her time with us. We look forward to meeting you and to welcoming your child.

continued

Tear off

Please tick the boxes that apply to you and add any comments you wish at the end.

	Yes	No
Would you like to come into school to meet _____'s teacher		
Is a late afternoon meeting suitable?		
Do you prefer an evening slot?		
Will you bring other children who need supervision?		
Would you like to discuss the nursery curriculum?		
Have you particular concerns about how your child will settle at school?		
Would you like to share your ideas/concerns before the actual meeting to allow us to prepare? If, for example, you wished to see a plan for the teaching year or know our policy on inclusion or bullying or supporting children with English as an additional language or other additional learning needs, we would like to be ready to share the appropriate documents with you or have consulted the appropriate specialists in advance.	*	*
NB. Please let us know of any medical conditions your child has, how we can help and, if appropriate, please give us a letter giving permission for the school nurse to administer medication.		
Please comment in the boxes * and * if you wish		

	Skill	Contribution
Have you a skill, e.g. baking, that you would enjoy sharing with the children in the nursery?		
If so, perhaps you would like to plan how you could contribute, e.g. on two mornings per month?		

Why should this be the case? One possibility is that both parents and teachers may feel vulnerable and be unsure how to proceed. In the early stages particularly, before a trust relationship has been established, many parents find it almost impossible to discuss their child's difficulties without becoming emotional, then embarrassed by being so. Very often they leave a consultation 'not really hearing what the teacher was saying' (parent of a child who was very disruptive in school).

Some parents fear that there will be an implied accusation of poor parenting skills and are supersensitive to suggestions, seeing them as criticism. Others may be resentful of attempts to change their children. 'Why do you try to make them different people?', asked Jill, who had two autistic sons. 'They aren't going to be "normal" in the way society defines normality, and they won't learn normality from other children, so why don't you adjust to them instead of always wanting to have them suit you?' This was quite an extreme response, but one that gave the school staff pause for thought. Were they wrong in what they were trying to do – which in effect was to make the two children fit a mould of their choosing? Was society wrong in not welcoming differences?

This question was debated at staff meetings. The practical strategies were as follows:

► An attempt would be made to recognise the profile of barriers each child had and to build on the child's strengths. This would be done by recognising the child's preferred way of learning and adapting teaching to suit.

► As most children learn best visually, the aim was to find where more visual material might be used, perhaps by having more pictures available at story time, or by preparing laminated cards that gave pictorial instructions on how to work the computer and showed the sequence of events for snack time.

► A chill-out room would be provided where soft background music would be played to calm the children at times of stress.

► The children would be observed closely and immediate positive reinforcement given when progress was made.

► Differentiated 'small steps' work appropriate to the children's needs would be provided.

The issue of the best ways to adapt regular teaching to break down barriers was to be raised at a later meeting once readings on Asperger's syndrome and autism had been shared. (See Chapter 10.)

FREYA

Listen to Amanda, mother of Freya, aged 3½. She was totally positive about her experience. She explained:

Although Freya is well behind the other children [a diagnosis would be global developmental delay], the teacher was so warm and she greeted me saying, 'Freya will be an asset to this nursery'. I was completely taken aback. The whole interview was positive and I left walking on air. The teacher explained that Freya would learn to play with other children and develop skills even though it would take a little longer than with the other children. She explained that new learning would always be geared to her strengths. We hadn't thought that strangers would think in terms of strengths, so that was wonderful.

The teacher also explained that for some of the day young people from the Secondary called 'Helping Hands' would come in to work with Freya. They would give her one-to-one attention following guidance from the teacher. The nursery staff thought she would enjoy young people helping her. They also pointed out that there were always adults in the outside area to stop her being knocked over and others on duty at lunchtime to check that she did eat. It all seemed too good to be true!

When the teacher asked me if I'd like to come into school, I thought about it, then decided that if Freya could cope, it would be better for her if I stayed at home. If a child is very slow to learn, then parents are always there. In this caring nursery we felt we could safely leave her and she would learn to be less dependent. That's what we hope, anyway.

JAKE

Listen now to Angie and Ben. They were parents who wanted to be just that and were increasingly annoyed by the school's repeated attempts to involve them. They explained:

As long as Jake is happy and getting along fine, we prefer to keep out and let the experts handle whatever crops up. We make sure he has his lunch box and give him money if there's a school trip. What more can we do? We both work all day and no one comes into the shop to help me serve the customers free of charge. Anyhow, they'd just get in the way. By the time I told them what to do, I could have done it myself, and I'm sure the same will be the case in schools. Teachers have enough to do, I should have thought. We also have to look after two sets of elderly parents, so thank you but no, we don't want to help in school.

Several parents were sceptical that such an innovation was necessary or desirable. They doubted whether their children wanted them in the nursery, and preferred to stay back. Typical reasons were that they wished:

- ▶ 'to give the children some freedom';
- ▶ 'to let them make mistakes without us looking over their shoulders all the time';
- ▶ 'to give the children something to tell us at teatime';
- ▶ 'to give us a break – we have them all the time';
- ▶ 'time to work – we have to earn!'.

Despite this, many parents, especially those who had children with additional learning needs, welcomed the opportunity to become more involved, and gave some evaluations of their time in the nursery. Listen to their views:

- ▶ 'It's really good. You can go along and meet other parents who have children who have a whole range of difficulties. We can have a cup of tea and relax. I made friends with people I'd never met before and I was able to tell them about support groups for children with ADHD.'
- ▶ 'I've never done anything like this before and I feel great. I go in to help with baking. The teacher gives me money and I do the shopping and bring the stuff back to school. I do that in the morning and the school gives me enough for a coffee in the café to say thank you, then later I set up the baking room. The children think I'm another teacher. No one has given me so much respect before. I just love it!'
- ▶ 'When you have a child who is different, you think you are the only one, and you wonder what others are thinking. You feel isolated, especially when they are 3 or 4, because there's very little help; you just have to get on with it. Now I realise that

there are children living round about who have difficulties too and I can meet up with their parents to chat over issues. It's not so bad now.'

In Chapter 1, Kim talked about drip-feeding information about a potential special need when the parents were unaware that such news was in the offing. She advised the following process:

Say to the parent, 'Do you ever notice [whatever the difficulty is]?' If the parents say 'no', then ask them to focus on particular instances that mirror those in nursery which have given cause for concern. If the child is asked to put his bag on the table and he runs to put it on the peg where it usually stays, then, if this kind of mistake happens regularly, the child is either not hearing the instruction or not understanding what has been said. Both hearing and comprehension need to be checked.

If the problem persists, at least the possibility of a learning difficulty has been raised and the staff (or SENCO) can ask permission to begin a referral process. Again this can be couched in terms of 'let's find out what we can do to support the child; there may be nothing wrong but because referrals take so long, it's best to err on the safe side'.

Some of the complexities of involving parents have been visited. In the past few years, much more recognition has been given to parents as first educators. Now they have been called 'the best therapists' (broadcast on autism by Dr Jamie Nicholls, 1 June 2004). They have a wealth of practical strategies to help their child. Listening to them and taking their well-tested strategies on board is surely the best way to nurture the child?

SOME STRATEGIES SUGGESTED BY PARENTS

Barbara first:

Jill is nearly 4 and has very poor balance. If the toilet is too high and her feet aren't firm on the floor, then she can't sit on the toilet without falling over. When she feels insecure, she gets up before she's done and gets all wet. At home we have a foam cushion to support her back. She likes to do everything herself and can manage fine if she's not rushed.

(The nursery copied the cushion pattern and made sure it was in place for Jill, who then managed much better.)

Then Fred explained:

Pete never feels the cold, and if he gets too warm he'll just strip off. This happens in two seconds, so be warned! Don't worry if he wants to go outside in a T-shirt when everyone else has to put a coat on. He does this at home. If you try to force him to wear a jacket, he'll scream. He can't tolerate heat at all.

Jay had another problem that helped the staff understand Randy's difficulties. She explained:

We have just fostered Randy, so he has had a lot of changes in his short life. He is away from his Mum, who is very ill, and although Randy was pretty deprived of material things at home, he is missing his family and constantly cries to go home. We are doing our best, but it's hard. If he doesn't behave very well, please understand what he's going through.

So, parents and foster-carers have a whole range of concerns about their children. Sharing ideas and plans can help avert any unnecessary misunderstandings and provide explanations of why children behave a little differently from their peers.

Part II

Understanding specific difficulties

Chapter 4

'Just let me play!'
Observing children at play

This chapter is written in response to 4-year-old Ronan's request, 'Just let me play'. He was attending a nursery where learning letters and numbers was given priority. His reaction, however, will confirm many parents' and practitioners' fears that in some settings, Primary 1 or Key Stage 1 goals have become part of the nursery ethos. New advice in England that there has to be more time for play comes as a relief to all those strongly in favour of a child-centred curriculum where the children learn through play. This is especially important for children who need additional learning support.

Let's consider what Ronan really missed when he didn't get to play:

▶ Being free to do what he liked when he liked?
▶ Choosing activities he enjoyed and which he could succeed at?
▶ Pretending he was someone else, somewhere else?
▶ A chance to practise the activities of daily living as well as the skills taught in the classroom, at his own pace?
▶ A break from concentrating and having to complete a task?
▶ Being free to do nothing if he so chose?
▶ Not having someone tell him how to do it better?

These would seem to be totally appropriate descriptors of time without stress – that is, time to play. Most researchers and authors, such as Cohen (1996), House (2002) and Macintyre and McVitty (2003), and almost all the children who were asked whether they would like more time to play, endorsed the suggestion wholeheartedly. They screamed 'YES!'.

Four-year-old Hamish from Aberdeen, who has ADHD, was one who was in no doubt. He enthused:

Aye, I like to play wi' the loons. I'd like to play al' day and no' go to nursery at all. I'd play at footie, an' dicin' a ba' an' that and then I'd gan' tae America in ma faither's boat.

(For non-Aberdonians, Hamish would prefer to play ball with other boys instead of going to nursery and then he'd go off in his father's fishing boat to America!)

What, then, are the skills that children learn as they play? The answer is that they have the opportunity to develop competences right across the learning spectrum. They develop:

▶ Social competence – through learning to share toys and ideas, to take turns and to wait till another child has finished their turn; to interact with children and adults who perhaps want them to do other things.

▶ Movement competence – through practising their fine and gross motor skills. They learn to control their bodies on the climbing frame, to place the pieces in a jigsaw puzzle, to thread beads and to move around without bumping into obstacles that are in the way.

▶ Intellectual competence – through suggesting ideas, engaging in role play, through remembering yesterday's 'good time' and concentrating hard to develop the idea further. They can also develop their imaginative skills as they enter their fantasy world and learn new vocabulary to support their ploy.

▶ Emotional competence – through being successful because they have set the parameters of their game. Through play they develop a positive sense of self and begin to be reflective and self-evaluative. They learn that other children have feelings too, and develop altruism and empathy – that is, willingness to care for others, even at some cost to themselves.

They can choose what they wish to do and develop their ideas as the play goes on. Moreover, they can do so at a pace that suits their level of competence. Freed of pressure to complete an activity or 'to do it better', they can enjoy playing alone, with friends, indoors and out, with resources of their choice or with none.

Why is learning through play so fruitful? The answer is that when children learn something new, they compare features of that new thing to activities and experiences they have already encountered, and they build on this to accomplish a new skill (see also Chapter 7). If the gap between the old and the new is not too large, learning is eased and more likely to be held in the short-term or working memory. Further similar experiences or repetition can enable it to be retained in the long-term memory ready to be recalled whenever appropriate. Of course children have to learn things that are quite different from anything they have done before, but, initially at least, this tends to be through rote learning that does not necessarily embrace the meaning of what is learned. (Learning times tables parrot-fashion without really understanding the meaning of the transactions would be an example of this.)

The important thing is that, especially at the start of a new year before relationships are established, nursery staff do not know what background experiences the children have had. So, if *they* select the things that are to be learned, the likelihood is that they will be inappropriate or the information will be learned through rote learning. The children of course expect the practitioners to know everything about them, such as where Auntie Jane lives and the name of her cat, so they don't see the need to explain. A much richer learning scenario becomes possible when any intervention from the practitioners is based on observation to find what kind of intervention, if any, is required. But this is time-consuming and often difficult to complete in a busy nursery, so observation schedules have to be prepared in advance or sticky labels or Post-its have to be at the ready so that continuous, detailed dated recordings in different contexts can be made. In this type of recording, practitioners can begin with a blank paper and note down exactly what occurs. Alternatively, they can set out to note instances of one competence across different tasks so that evidence of ability or difficulty in one skill demonstrated in different environments is gathered.

It helps too if each member of staff is responsible for observing just one or two children for a spell and then the staff are rotated so that different eyes confirm observations or add information about progress or regression over time. As a result of the amassed 'evidence' at staff discussion time, strategies to overcome difficulties can be shared and evaluated. This process can help less experienced practitioners to make the most appropriate intervention.

It is important that enough detail is noted to make the recording 'useful'. The child's age is important, as different levels of skill can be expected as the children mature. The date is vital too, because it enables practitioners to monitor progress over time and shows whether practice and maturation are having an effect. It is also important to know

49

Lauren, age 4 yrs 2 months: 16.1.04

She is engrossed in building a zoo, selecting wild animals from the box. She counts them out (up to 6) and then tells me how fierce they are. She lines them up in size order and then asks Mar, 'Have you got cages?'

This was after the nursery outing to the zoo.

Alex, age 3 yrs 5 months: 16.1.04

*Check Alex's hand and finger strength

Alex still makes wispy drawings (in file) and avoids the writing table altogether. She cannot do up buttons and clutches small items into her body rather than using the pincer grip. She looks strained and her hands are small and fragile.

Action:
Put out Theraputty/Play-Doh at the crafts table. Encourage pulling and moulding. Check with SENCO. Physiotherapy required?

■ **FIGURE 4.1** Sticky-label recordings of observations of Lauren and Alex. The label for Lauren was completed in her first week at nursery to find the kinds of activities she chose to do

who made the observation, because even when criteria are set out, observers may have different levels of expertise in making assessments. It can be very revealing when two observers compare their recordings about the same event! This is why different observers should view the same child, especially if difficulties are suspected.

For example, the first recording in Figure 4.1 shows that Lauren was able to concentrate, she had retained knowledge about different animals and she could count. She could interact confidently with Marie and was willing for her to join her game. She was also planning to extend her play (to build cages) and was competent in asking an adult for different resources. *Staff response:* Set out factual books about animals. Provide rocks and toys for the water tray so that the children might consider penguins in their habitat.

The second recording was made to check one particular competence that had been giving the practitioners cause for concern. This was a specific recording in which the assessor concentrated on gathering evidence across different activities and making suggestions about the support that was required. Similar recordings were made each day so that a bank of evidence was ready to show other professionals *if* referral became necessary.

INVOLVING PARENTS IN OBSERVATION

At a staff meeting (see Chapter 3), the question of parents overseeing children at play had been raised as a possible meaningful involvement. Would parents also be able to make useful observations if they were provided with competences to assess? The parents understood that not all competences might be observed during a single day.

Please complete the following observation schedule for Sharon. Please tick the appropriate boxes.

Name: Sharon; Age: 4 yrs 4 months; Date: 14.6.02; Parent's name: A. Hannay	Yes, can do	Some difficulty	Cannot do it
Can crawl			X
Can stand and sit still (balance check)			X
Can pick up small objects using the pincer grip	X		
Is sure which hand gives the best results	X		
Can climb on the frame		X	
Can cope independently at the toilet		X	
Can balance on a wide bench	X		
Can control a pencil	X		

FIGURE 4.2 A first observation schedule for parents

From this chart, it was apparent that while Sharon's fine motor skills were good, she had difficulty with co-ordination and balance – that is, in being still. The surprise came in noting that her balance on the bench was good. Her dynamic balance – that is, while she was moving – was more developed than her static balance.

51

Action

This finding showed that the practitioners should concentrate on developing Sharon's body awareness so that she would learn about poise in standing and sitting still.

This success of this idea stimulated Rhona, a practitioner particularly interested in assessment and recording to list 'things it would be useful to know'.

What sorts of things did she decide it would it be appropriate for parents to record? She consulted the documents *Curriculum Guidance for the Foundation Stage* (DfEE 2000) and *A Curriculum framework for Children 3–5* (SCCC 1999) to identify key competences (see also Appendix 1). After discussion with her colleagues, her list was set out and shared with the parents, and the first trial began. Rhona decided that subdividing the competences that parents were to observe into the four aspects of development made sense, because then recording would encompass all aspects of learning. The following list was compiled.

Motor competence

Are the children:

▶ able to move confidently with balance, co-ordination and control?
▶ able to crawl?
▶ using the pincer grip to pick up and let go?
▶ using a dominant hand/foot?
▶ able to use a variety of equipment/apparatus?
▶ able to sit and stand still (the hardest movement of all)?

Social competence

Are the children:

▶ willing to share resources?
▶ taking turns?
▶ caring for other children?
▶ supporting someone with difficulties?

Intellectual competence

Are the children:

▶ involved in imaginative play?
▶ listening to and acting on each other's suggestions?
▶ making appropriate suggestions to take the play forward?
▶ staying with an activity until something was achieved?
▶ following instructions adequately?

Emotional competence

Are the children:

▶ staying reasonably calm throughout any 'upset', such as having toys taken away by other children or leaving their mother?
▶ being resilient — for example, settling down quickly after a disappointment?
▶ understanding other children's feelings?
▶ coping with a change in routine?
▶ able to behave appropriately in different settings?

Interaction competence

Are the children:

▶ initiating a conversation?
▶ listening to what was being said?
▶ responding (in speech and action) appropriately, showing comprehension?
▶ articulating clearly?
▶ using pronouns correctly?

Understanding and using non-verbal signs (eye contact, gestures)

Are the children:

▶ beckoning for help?
▶ pointing out — showing, demonstrating an action?
▶ offering a toy to another child?

53 ■

▶ using gestures to reject another's approach?

▶ hitting out, showing aggression?

▶ making repeated inappropriate noises, e.g. echolalia (repeating mechanically words just spoken by someone else).

Developing richer observational data

Rhona's evaluation of her scheme was that she wanted to alert the parents to the potential of crossing the boundaries between different aspects of development to give a fuller picture of children's maturation and progress. She provided the following example based on Lauren's play with animals.

Example shared with parents

The nursery curriculum is subdivided into five areas, and these provide a number of learning outcomes that are used to guide teaching, the provision of resources and the kinds of assessments that should be made. So, it is possible to set out to observe the incidence of one or two skills. The more experienced practitioners, however, will be able to observe much more as they follow the children. Indeed, they may find that the children have achieved a learning outcome different from the intended one as they play. Thus, instead of limiting observations to one aspect of development, it is possible to show achievement right across the board. An example of possibilities is given in Figure 4.3.

As the observations are being made, practitioners are also looking out for developments that happen as a result of the activity. Reflections they might centre on questions – for example, does the interest in animals lead them to:

▶ paint stripes like a tiger?

▶ make eggs with dough?

▶ slither like a snake?

▶ create masks at the gluing table?

▶ seek for factual books on animals?

▶ take an animal story sac home?

▶ develop new vocabulary?

It can be seen that observations are based in play experiences but implicitly can encompass all aspects of development and learning.

Child's name: Lauren and Sally	Observers: Jo and Petra Points to observe	Extended observations
Activity: playing with zoo animals	*Intellectual development*, e.g. Selection of appropriate animals for zoo	Descriptive language e.g. colour; patterns on coats; camouflage Length /quality of interactions e.g. number/length of questions
	Social development, Ability to share Willingness to take turns Leadership	Body language; facial expressions showing reactions to suggestions
	Emotional development, Willingness to follow suggestions Temperament	Willingness to contribute Reaction to having ideas rejected Vulnerable; resilient; domineering, passive?
	Motor development, Handling animals – picking up using the pincer grip Ability to let go – to place the animals without them falling over.	Animal movements, e.g. bounding, creeping, flying, tracking, swooping, hovering, flitting etc.

FIGURE 4.3 Observations of children's achievement across the board

The children's immediate responses and continued interests all demonstrate their learning.

Note that observers must be careful to limit their assessments according to the findings from the observations. Care must be taken to avoid assuming things that are not based on evidence.

USING VIDEO AS AN OBSERVATIONAL TOOL

After several episodes, discussions compared a clutch of observational data (sticky label recordings and time sampling taken by parents and practitioners). These findings were analysed and interpreted by the

■ TABLE 4.1 Advantages and disadvantages of using video as an observational tool

Advantages	Disadvantages
Makes an accurate record	Procedural bias: children may alter their behaviour for the film
Sequential recordings can show progress/regression over time	Background noise may prevent accurate transcription of talk
No personal bias invalidates the data	Time-consuming to analyse – still depends on the assessor's ability to 'see'
The film can be replayed often to check first impressions and look for other items	The child may go out of range, so the video may miss incidents that are revealing and important

Source: C. Macintyre, *The Art of Action Research in the Classroom*. London: David Fulton, 2000

practitioners at staff discussion time. As a result of ambiguities in deciding what the children's behaviours might indicate – out of context, it was difficult to be precise – a video camera was set up, and, after some time, when the children were ignoring its presence, recording began. An investigation into the benefits of video recording showed that there were both advantages and disadvantages in using this method of gathering data.

OBSERVATION LEADING TO INTERVENTION

Observing play is much more complex than it sounds. The observing must be unobtrusive, yet it is difficult to stay back if children are struggling to achieve. However, adult intervention can so easily change the game and render the children powerless. One of the ongoing and turbulent discussions concerns the role of the adult in children's play. Should children's play be structured and supported by adults so that they can 'progress', or is that intrusion acting against the development of intangible but important skills such as self-direction, or even the development of fantasy? Cohen (1996) is only one of those who despair when he hears of 'social engineers on the swings'!

Making assumptions about what the children are thinking and feeling also has to be avoided, especially when one is observing children with additional needs. This is because adults tend to interpret what they see in the light of their own experience, and this could be quite different from the child's intention.

Listen to Fiona, who had volunteered to help children with communication difficulties:

> When I said I would like to help children with additional learning needs, I was given Sandy as my focus child. I was told that as he was on the autistic spectrum, he wouldn't be able to communicate with me. Well, he came right up to me and asked, 'What kind of car do you have?' I thought, 'What's this, I've made contact, he likes me', and I felt very pleased. When the teachers sat down to evaluate the session, however, and I explained what had happened, the teacher in charge explained that Sandy wasn't holding a conversation, he was repeating a phrase that he used whenever he met someone new. I was so disappointed and realised I hadn't communicated with him as I'd thought. The next day he ran up to me again and said exactly the same thing. When I tried to stop him running away, he squirmed out of my grasp and jumped on top of the washing machine, which was churning away in the corner. He just loved to watch the dishcloths getting washed.

Could play help the emotional development of children like Sandy? Elkind (1991) highlighted this critically important aspect of development when he wrote, 'Play is young children's only defence against the many real or imagined attacks and slights they encounter. Play is always a transformation of reality in the service of the self.' It is tremendously encouraging if play experiences can act as sublimation so that the hurts of the day can be diminished. As most children with learning difficulties experience negative interactions at best, and bullying, verbal and even physical, at worst, Elkind has provided a strong rationale for the inclusion of 'times to play' for these children. Isaacs identified this kind of benefit many years ago when she claimed, 'In play the child is recreating elements in past situations which can embody his emotional or intellectual need' (1930: 425). This being so, skilled observation can identify aspects that have disturbed the child and that can, through careful intervention, be put right.

Lauri's nursery teacher gave an example. She described one scenario that would clarify Isaac's assertion.

> When Lauri's new baby brother arrived, we were on the lookout for any change in behaviour, as we knew she was a highly strung child.

57

Her parents had described her as 'very bright and sensitive'. After the baby arrived, she became surly and aggressive, hitting other children and not responding to any offers of comfort from us. She had always enjoyed the home area, but now she wouldn't go near it. Things got worse and worse till she didn't speak at all. The breakthrough came when we turned the home area into a hospital and she joined in 'making a sick doll better'. When we told her mum about this and suggested that perhaps the corner had been turned, a light flashed across her face. It appeared that at home Lauri had tried to hurt the baby and refused to say she was sorry, and 'the whole episode had spiralled out of control. We were up three times in the night, tired out, and finished up yelling at Lauri. We realised this was a no-win situation, but we didn't seem able to resolve it. When we tried to explain that a tiny baby needs lots of attention, she froze us out.' The teacher was sure that Lauri's effort in 'making the doll better' had acted as compensation and helped relieve her feelings of guilt and anxiety.

Rawson and Rose (2002) continue this theme with their claim that 'the life processes e.g. moral competence and conscience are all developed through play'. But what of children like Sandy, children who cannot imagine or pretend, such as children with autism and those with very poor short-term memories who may not recap earlier episodes? Do they have no conscience? Can they benefit from having time to play?

Listen to Denny, a teacher of children with autism in a special school who tackled this question. He told of his experience:

Our children are quite profoundly disabled, and while they can play with toys, they don't engage in imaginative play or play with each other. In fact, some of the children will take their favourite toys and go to their own corner and not want to budge. Alex immediately searches for his red truck, but he doesn't make it run along roads or carry loads. He puts the truck close to his ear and makes the wheels spin. He is fascinated by things that go round and round. The children can be very protective of their own things and go off the planet if anyone tries to change them over in an attempt to enlarge their understanding of different objects. I suppose that's because they don't really understand sharing or taking turns and they depend heavily on things being the same. At snack times they know they have to share biscuits and drinks, but that seems to be a routine that they've learned over a long time. Sadly, they don't seem able to transfer that learning to other experiences.

Denny offered an explanation of the children's difficulties:

Not being able to imagine is really at the root of not being able to play. If you can't understand how another person is feeling, then it's impossible to anticipate how they will react, and so how can two children play together?

He also raised the idea of there being underlying competences that have to be present to allow children to play. Does this mean that there is a hierarchy of demands that children with different conditions might not aspire to meet?

Children pass through different developmental stages in their play. Identifying and recording what children with support needs can do as they play could provide a useful assessment checklist and help observers judge whether intervention is appropriate and, if so, what form it should take.

Both indoor and outdoor play (especially if there are various re-sources, such as a tent, a climbing frame, fallen branches or large blocks to build a hideaway), provide key opportunities for observation. This is the best way to recognise whether a child can initiate or participate in an imaginative game.

THE DEVELOPMENT OF IMAGINATIVE PLAY

Self-directed imaginative play is crucial for children's emotional and social development, and most children, given the chance, are enriched by entering a fantasy world and imagining happenings there. By so doing they begin to make comparisons and gain a stronger sense of themselves (who I am) and how they might cope in a very different environment. Even reflecting on yesterday and anticipating tomorrow depends on imagination, because it depends on being able to conjure up images of events not happening now. Children with autism find this impossible (see the video *The Problem Is Understanding*, produced by the National Autistic Society).

'Getting to play' is fulfilling because there is no sense of having to meet some predisposed standard, and there should be no adult there

59

telling children how to do it. Susan Isaacs (1933) wrote, 'Play is a child's life and the means by which he comes to understand the world around him'. She was emphasising the intellectual development that is implicit when children play. Sixty years later, Cohen (1996) put his finger on the realism of adult intervention when he asked, 'How can we, long out of touch oldies, tell children how to play?'. How indeed?

It seems very strange, then, that educational literature urges practitioners to 'structure children's spontaneous play'! (DfEE 2000) To do this without spoiling the thought processes of the child, the practitioners would need insights into the child's thinking and a clear idea of what was in the child's mind. Otherwise, the spontaneity will be spoiled and the ownership of the play episode is taken from the child. Yet practitioners often feel it is imperative to intrude. Very often they are conditioned to ask questions without really knowing what they are to do with the answers! By so doing, they intimate that they have a better way and that they do not trust the child to play successfully by him- or herself!

IS PLAYING ALWAYS FUN?

Many children with additional learning needs find it difficult to play. The freedom can overwhelm them. Structure has gone, there is a cacophony of noise and movement, there is too much space, which can be frightening, and the games that others play may be beyond the skill or comprehension or imaginative level of those who have difficulties. Worst of all, it gives the opportunity for bullies to taunt and to make life extremely difficult. To ascertain each child's problem, observations can usefully be subdivided into the different aspects of development.

Social difficulties include:

▶ not being allowed to join in;
▶ not knowing how to get into a game;
▶ ignoring invitations to join in;
▶ not being able to follow the 'rules' that someone else has set;
▶ not being able to read non-verbal signals and therefore not understanding what to do.

Physical/movement difficulties include:

▶ not having the strength or mobility to participate;
▶ getting out of breath and not being able to keep up;

▶ being allergic to playground spaces – for example, proximity to grass, flowers, rapeseed oil;

▶ flapping the hands or making other strange, off-putting movements that deter any approach from other children.

Sensorimotor difficulties include:

▶ not having the physical control to be still and to move slowly;

▶ not having the balance and/or co-ordination or speed of movement to allow participation in a game;

▶ poor body and spatial awareness, resulting in bumping and barging;

▶ not being able to catch or kick a ball.

Emotional difficulties include:

▶ not being able to imagine what is going on and what might happen;

▶ not having the confidence to make suggestions;

▶ low tolerance of being touched – for example, not being able to hold hands in a ring;

▶ having no empathy or altruism – no willingness to help others;

▶ exhibiting compulsive repetitive behaviours;

▶ not being able to wait and listen.

Intellectual difficulties include:

▶ not knowing what to do;

▶ having poor short-term memory, or no recall of previous games;

▶ not being able to make suggestions as to how the game could progress;

▶ not being able to plan or organise resources to fulfil the plan.

Observing play can show which children are loners, isolated from the main body of children. When they can't explain what is wrong, it can be very difficult to know how to help. Providing them with alternative experiences may be the best way until confidence is gained.

To help children play, Bee (2001) always recommends finding the children's main interest and encouraging those with the same interests to play together. This did not work for Alan, who has behavioural difficulties. 'He is a very intelligent boy,' explained Tom, his teacher, 'and he is one step ahead of us, so that when we notice an interest and try to follow it up, he knows exactly what we are trying to do; he switches off and he isn't interested any more. He would do anything rather than try to please us.'

Tom considered that this finding held a key lesson for intervention, which was 'Stay back, don't do it; trust the children to know what's best for them. With the best will in the world, intervention can spoil what's going on. Just let the children play!'.

Play can:

▶ provide a time of freedom, an opportunity to do something or nothing, and so reduce stress;

▶ allow the children to make decisions about what they would like to do without having to justify or explain what or why;

▶ allow them to abandon the play scenario at will;

▶ provide enjoyment and relaxation;

▶ enhance learning because of the skills and understandings that may develop;

▶ encourage fantasy and the development of the imagination;

▶ develop social interaction and communication;

▶ confuse and distress some children through not having routine and structure.

When play can do all these things, and moreover it is the children's first choice, then surely adults cannot deny young children the chance to learn through play?

Chapter 5

Understanding speech and language difficulties

When most children come into nursery, they are able to chat with adults and friends, and they have developed a large vocabulary of words that convey wishes and ideas and give explanations. Some children, even at the age of 3, can enter the realms of fantasy and show by their expressive use of words that they are developing a wonderful imagination. Adults have to be able to join in, in order to extend the children's learning, but this is an extremely demanding task, one that is open to derision by the children if it is not gauged correctly! But sadly, not all children can cope at this level of talk.

What kinds of observations give rise to a suspicion that a speech and language difficulty might be on the cards? Indicators would be children:

▶ who are willing to talk but whose poor articulation means they cannot be understood;

▶ who never approach an adult or start a conversation;

▶ who look blank and do not follow instructions, or always mutter, 'don't know';

▶ who don't understand turn-taking and/or speak out of context – that is, have a one-sided conversation and/or have difficulty keeping the rhythm of a conversation;

▶ who will offer a short statement but who won't follow up an adult's attempt to extend what they say;

▶ who appear baffled if another child tries to start a conversation with them;

▶ who have to watch others to see what to do, rather than listen and act on their own initiative.

It can be seen, then, that language development is complex. It depends on the integration of several underlying skills:

▶ learning to make speech sounds;
▶ listening to hear speech sounds;
▶ understanding the meaning of words;
▶ understanding rhythm within words and phrases;
▶ being able to link words together.

Then, in holding a conversation, children must cope with:

▶ turn-taking – waiting, interjecting, responding quickly;
▶ listening and making sense of another's pitch and speed of sound;
▶ holding eye contact;
▶ paying attention to the topic being talked about;
▶ adopting the body language to match the words;
▶ reading the body language of the talker;
▶ adapting the level of language to the recipients' level of understanding.

Adopting appropriate body language and being able to read that of others are important, because 90 per cent of the meaning of a conversation comes through non-verbal communication – that is, through postures, gestures and facial expressions. If, for example, a nursery practitioner wants to praise a child and says, 'What a lovely colourful picture' but at the same time looks away to observe another child, then the body language signals that the painting is of less importance and may not be so good after all! Situations like this, where verbal and non-verbal communication disagree, are examples of meta-incongruence, and can be a major source of confusion for both children and adults.

But of course learning to converse doesn't happen at once. There is a developmental process. Understanding the stages (see Table 5.1) can help nursery staff determine the level of delay or difference.

Bowerman (1985) underpins this process when she explains, 'When language starts to come in, it does not introduce new meanings to the child. Rather it is used to express only those meanings the child has already formulated, independent of language'. In effect, she is highlighting the contribution of experiences to the acquisition of language. In the nursery, the plethora of activities and experiences could be justified by this explanation alone.

■ TABLE 5.1 A developmental plan for speaking

Age	Words	Stories	Activities
5 years	Clear articulation; compound phrases	Can retell a story; suggest new ideas Can sequence three pictures Can use pronouns correctly	Can empathise with others' feelings; understands rules and routines
4 years	Seeks explanations. Asks When? Why? Can visualise events elsewhere	Enjoys repetition and contributing known phrases to stories	Can role-play; can understand characterisation
3 years	Uses sentences of 4–5 words Complex use of words	Will listen, adapt and recast sentences	Joins in songs and rhymes Beats rhythms
2 years	Huge increase in vocabulary – the naming explosion Links two words, e.g. love you, go away	Follows stories – recognises favourite characters and routines Gesture and body language combined – holophrases Communication strategies used, e.g. motherese (higher-pitched simplified language)	Asserts independence – tantrums Telegraphic speech, i.e. uses only essential words, e.g. 'I going.'
1 year	Monosyllabic babbling: da, da, da Understanding evident from facial expression and gestures	Understands simple instructions, e.g. come here Can convey wishes through gestures Understands 50 words: makes own words for wants Words learned slowly at this pre-linguistic stage.	Enjoys peekaboo (the basis of turn-taking) Memory and a sense of self are developing

Clear articulation, the basis of spoken communication, is often the first assessment that nursery practitioners make. This depends on phonological processes – that is, sound rules. These affect the pronunciation of similar sounds. Such sounds are affected by where they are produced in the mouth. Even nursery-age children can be made aware of where in the mouth sounds should be made, and they can be helped to practise the correct places.

SOME SOUNDS YOUNG CHILDREN FIND DIFFICULT

▶ The sounds that should be made at the back of the mouth are produced further forward (fronting), so 'car' becomes 'tar'.

▶ Sounds that should be made at the front of the mouth are made further back (backing), so 'dog' becomes 'gog'.

▶ Shortening of sounds occurs when fricatives, e.g. f, v, z, s, th, br, are shortened so that 'bread' becomes 'bed' and 'shop' becomes 'pop'.

These differences give rise to smiles when the children are very young, and parents are reading their facial expressions and body language to understand the talk in context. However, out of context and when the mispronunciations are retained beyond the age when they should have been outgrown, such difficulties may cause confusion and bewilderment, and the children must be helped.

Some sounds *are* more difficult to formulate than others. When should each be acquired? Burnett and Frame (2003) have produced a table, 'The steps in acquiring speech sounds', that could be very useful as a checklist (Table 5.2).

But what of children who do not follow this maturational pathway? It is time to consider speech and language difficulties.

SPEECH AND LANGUAGE IMPAIRMENT

When difficulties persist, the children are said to have speech and language impairment. A *specific language impairment* (SLI) has different forms and different causes. It encompasses different names, such as developmental language delay and developmental language disorder. These are often used interchangeably, although 'delay' and 'disorder' are key words in indicating different conditions. SLI is a term that describes children who

TABLE 5.2 The steps in acquiring
speech sounds

Chronological age (years)	Speech sounds
1.5–3	p m h n
1.5–4	b c k g d
1.5–6	t ng
2.5–4	f y
3–7	s z
3–7.5	ch sh
3–8	r l
4–7	j
4–8	v
4.5–8	th
6–8.5	zh

only demonstrate difficulties in speech and language, so children who are deaf or whose language difficulty is caused by a physical problem such as a cleft palate, or an emotional one such as autism, are not included under this heading. In other words, 'SLI' is used to refer to a difficulty that is surprising given the child's other competences. The different manifestations of SLI pose problems for practitioners in the nursery, who must try to ascertain the root of any difficulty so that intervention can be appropriate. They must also assess whether expert 'outside' help should be sought. As speech and language are fundamental to all learning, requests for support need to be put in place as early as possible and whenever there is a doubt about proficiency.

In developmental language delay, the children continue to make the 'normal' mistakes in grammar or articulation beyond the time when they should be overtaken by more correct speech. Once the child's language does appear, however, it develops normally. The children catch up and all is well. Early worries are most often unfounded.

In children with a language disorder, however, the various aspects of language develop atypically. The disorder makes progress in language uneven and difficult. Communication is hampered, as are most other aspects of learning.

These explanations show why it is imperative to distinguish between the two conditions, although this is by no means an easy thing to do. Language delay may resolve itself, but it may turn out to be a disorder, requiring a speech and language therapist.

Support for developmental language delay and language disorder can be obtained from:

Royal College of Speech and Language Therapists (RCSLT)
2 White Hart Yard
London SE1 1NX

THE TIMING OF DECISIONS

In nursery, the question 'Is this a lasting difficulty or will maturation and experience of the setting be enough to make the problem go away?' continually raises its head. To confuse decision-making further, there are two sides to every interaction, and inexperienced practitioners may feel that *they* are closing down opportunities for extending children's talk by questioning, making inappropriate interventions or simply not knowing what to talk about. In cases like this, it is important that another adult is aware of the dilemma and takes a turn to listen and assess.

It can be very frustrating when other children understand a child and the supervising adults can't! But at least that child speaks, while a few just don't! Let's consider the different possibilities within SLI. Doing so will emphasise how difficult assessment is, especially when one kind of difficulty can permeate into others. This is why, when difficulties are not transitory, obtaining expert help is critically important. What, then, are the different types of difficulty?

DIFFERENT MANIFESTATIONS OF SPECIFIC LANGUAGE IMPAIRMENT

▶ The children understand what is being said (this is deduced by observing their responses to instructions or requests), but other people cannot understand their replies. They try to speak but cannot be understood. This may cause them to stop trying. Their problem is an articulation difficulty that may be caused by poor muscle tone in the mouth, the tongue and in the muscles that control breathing. Alternatively, a disorder such as glue ear may have prevented the children hearing clearly when speech was being internalised. Children with Down's syndrome often suffer this.

▶ The children do not understand what is being said, and their speech is confined to a few words. This is a comprehension and expressive language difficulty.

▶ The children can speak clearly and are happy to do so, but what they say is strange, showing that they are not following the purpose of the conversation. This causes others to pause or stop the interaction or to amend their line of thinking to try to reply appropriately. These children do not appreciate the 'rules' of conversation or they either do not listen to or do not understand what the other person says.

▶ The children speak, but use single words or short, disjointed sentences. Linking words are left out. At school age, this indicates a developmental delay.

These descriptors will show that it is useful to separate comprehension (whether language is understood) from expression (being able to use language). Most children will be stronger in one area or the other, although some difficulty may be found in both. Each child needs a planned individual programme of support. Unfortunately, difficulties can be missed. When Caris's mum met her after nursery and asked, 'Who did you play with today?', Caris replied, 'outside'. Her Mum only heard the play link and was content that the answer was correct. When Caris's inappropriate response was pointed out and more detailed listening followed, it became apparent that Caris was not attending to the full meaning of a question but instead was latching on to a familiar word.

But first, let's consider the children who choose not to speak at all.

Selective mutism

The term 'selective mutism' is used when children speak without difficulty in some situations yet maintain silence in others, usually in new venues and with people they do not know. It happens most often in nursery – that is, at the age of 3 to 5 – and, unusually, more girls than boys are affected. When failure to speak in some situation persists over two terms or so, the children can be said to have selective mutism. This is not caused by shyness or the children being lazy or antagonistic. It is a psychological problem where children freeze and become unable to speak – an extreme form of social anxiety.

Four-year-old Natalie is a case in point. She came into the nursery apparently at ease, collected the doll's pram and then would not be moved from her spot beside the radiator, where she stayed silent and brooding. No amount of persuasion would allow her to say what she would like for snack or whether she would enjoy a turn on the bike. Yet when she went home she chatted happily about all the things she had done and what the other children had said. Her parents were surprised, almost unbelieving that she had been silent all morning and, like the nursery staff, could not understand what was amiss.

The nursery staff asked Natalie's parents to tape some of her conversations at home, and the recording showed that she had no difficulty understanding or replying to chats they initiated at home. In the light of this evidence, the visiting speech and language therapist advised a 'wait and see' approach for a time and advised the staff to interact normally and not to draw attention to her difficulty. After five weeks she began to whisper to a friend, and from that time progress was slow but it was maintained.

Generally, progress is very slow in cases of selective mutism, and the children's personality trait of being sensitive and reticent stays with them. Where intervention is required, a psychologist and speech and language therapist will assess intelligence, verbal comprehension and, wherever possible, expressive speech. There are now specific treatments that can be given, so it is important that the experts are consulted when difficulties persist.

Further information can be obtained from:

Selective Mutism Information and Research Association (SMIRA)
13 Humberstone Drive
Leicester LE5 ORE
Tel: 0116 212 7411 or 020 7378 1200

Semantic and pragmatic disorders: clarifying the terms

Semantic – the meaning of words and phrases.
Pragmatic – knowing what to say when, i.e. how to use language in
   different situations.

Children with semantic and pragmatic disorders are identified by their unusual use or comprehension of speech. Often the children have difficulties with both these aspects, but they can occur singly, and for assessment in the early years they have to be considered separately.

Semantic difficulties result in children taking the literal meaning of a phrase. One autistic child, despite being a strong swimmer, nearly drowned because he had read a notice that said 'no swimming' (see the video *The Problem Is Understanding* from the National Autistic Society). This is an extreme case, but many other phrases interpreted literally result in no action. 'Can you open the door?' may win a nod but no move to comply. 'Pull your socks up' may result in the child doing just that, and one hopes that the children will never hear the words 'Get lost'.

Children with *pragmatic* difficulties find social interactions very difficult. They do not make the effort to extend conversations by using phatics (mmmm?), or they interrupt and bring conversations to a close. They may speak for too long and add irrelevant information.

Children with a semantic–pragmatic disorder may have a wide vocabulary and speak in well-constructed sentences. But they say more than they understand, and often fail to understand the meaning held within a conversation. Rapin and Allen (1987) explain that children thus affected use scripts in conversation – that is, they say the same words over and over again. How does one begin to explain the subtleties of language to a child who doesn't understand?

Information is available from:

Department of Speech and Language Therapy
University of Strathclyde
Jordanhill Campus
Glasgow G13 1PP

What advice can help practitioners who meet children with these difficulties?

▶ Have a conversation in a quiet spot where there are fewer distractors. Wait till the child is paying attention before beginning. Some children, perhaps most of them, can be very easily distracted, especially if they would rather be outside on the bike than speaking to you! So, choose the time and the place carefully. Talk about something the child has experienced or something that has been drawn or made. On no account say, 'What's that?'. Even phatics, such as 'Oh wow', suggesting

'Isn't that splendid?', are better, because they can cover the fact that you don't know!

▶ Give the children time to form a request or an answer. Avoid looking out beyond them or appearing agitated, because this suggests that you have other, more important things to do, such as supervising other children in the nursery. This can hassle the child into making inaccurate sounds.

TALKING WITH CHILDREN

To extend the children's talk, a good idea is to tell them about your own experiences, making sure of course that the children have had similar ones! So:

▶ Use reflective statements, not closed questions that only require one-word answers.

An example will clarify:

Practitioner: What did you do on your holiday?
Aidan: Nothing!

A more productive conversation can be stimulated by beginning with a reflective statement, e.g.

Practitioner: When I was little, for my holiday I used to go to the seaside and play on the sand.
Aidan: Me too, and there was crabs and things like in the book.
Teacher: I used to run away when I saw a crab.
Aidan: Well, if you were wee, you'd be scared, but big boys pick them up and put them in the rock pools. That's where they like – when it's warm and shallow water.

The more extended version led to the teacher sharing a book of seaside pictures with Aidan, and he was interested to develop his knowledge of rock pools and all the creatures that live in them.

▶ Avoid correcting mistakes in grammar or pronunciation. This will only prevent the child trying again and so learning the correct way. *Model* the correct way, giving a very slight emphasis to any word that was incorrect. Children need to have confidence and be relaxed to make changes.

If the child says, 'I like cool – fun', say quietly, 'I think it's good news that you enjoy school'. This is a gentle hint, but also shows the child that you understood what he was saying. This gives him confidence to try again.

If speech is really unclear, ask the parents to tell you what the child likes to do or what happened at the weekend so that there is some shared basis for a 'conversation'. After all, the child will expect you to know!

Have a fun activity, e.g. 'Let's all make "t" sounds to tell the tortoise we are coming up the path' or 'What did Mrs Mouse say when she found naughty Maurice had gone into the hole?'. 'She said "u, u, u, u"'. (See Appendix 2 for the full story, which has phrases for repetition.)

Giving instructions

▶ Be sure about the number of instructions that are implicit in one task. Simplify the task by providing *visual* clues for reference.

For example, 'Fetch your apron, wash your hands and then spread your biscuit for snack' houses three tasks. Two words, 'Snack time', can portray the whole routine if there is a sequence on the wall to show what comes first, second and third (Figure 5.1).

Similarly, 'Before you go outside you have to fetch your coat, put it on and do up the zip, then you can go'. This sequence can be replaced

FIGURE 5.1 Photo sequence to remind a child of the sequence of events at snack time

73

FIGURE 5.2 Photo sequence to remind a child of the sequence of events when putting on a coat before going out

with 'Outside time' when a photo sequence shows the correct order of events (Figure 5.2). The photographs give reminders of the sequence of actions and thereby save children having to memorise what comes first, then next, so relieving the stress of the day.

These ideas are useful for children who find following more than one instruction difficult. Children with dyslexia, dyspraxia, ADHD, Asperger's syndrome and Down's syndrome who learn most easily through visual modes all find that these visual sequences help them sequence their actions. The pictures also take away the stress of having to remember.

Chapter 6

Understanding movement difficulties

In Chapter 2, Simon explained his frustration at not being able to do the things he wanted to do. These were movement things, such as riding a bike or spreading toast at snack time. His skinned knees also bore evidence to the fact that he suffered many falls, showing that his balance and spatial awareness were poor. How important were his difficulties for Simon's future development? The answer must be, *critically important*, because movement underlies all learning. Anyone who doubts this might like to ponder the question 'How do you know children have learned if they don't move?'. After all, the first assessments children have are of their movement milestones, such as when they sit unsupported, if and when they crawl, when they walk, when they say their first words. The results are telling more than the timing of the acquisition of the basic movements patterns; they are indicating whether maturation is happening as it should and whether learning is happening apace. If doubts still persist about the value of being able to move effectively in different environments, then listing some nursery activities (Table 6.1) will show the part movement plays in early learning and perhaps convince doubters about its importance. Pointers for assessment are bracketed.

Many nursery-age children who have additional learning needs will have difficulties with one or several of these movements. They will be awkward and tend to bump into others and/or drop things. Typically they are clumsy children, although that descriptive term is no longer used because it has negative connotations, suggesting that if the children just tried harder or took more time or care, they could overcome their difficulties.

Sadly, this is not the case, because these children do not have the balance, co-ordination and control to make this improvement. They also lack body and spatial awareness, so they don't feel where their bodies

▨ TABLE 6.1 The part movement plays in early learning

Fine motor/manipulative skills	Gross motor skills
Picking up and letting go (use of the pincer/tripod grip)	Walking (poise and control of the limbs; ability to be still)
Talking (clear articulation)	Running (momentum and fluency in the action)
Writing, drawing and painting (controlling a pencil or brush)	Jumping (gauging the correct take-off point and the amount of height required)
Fastening buttons and zips (working at the midline of the body)	Crawling/climbing (cross-lateral co-ordination)
Spreading at snacktime (gauging the amount of strength needed to spread biscuits or toast)	Skipping (rhythm, balance and co-ordination)
Threading beads (precision and dexterity)	Combined actions: running and jumping (assessing the transitions between movements)
Mixing paint (two-handed co-ordination)	Riding a bike (balance, spatial awareness and control)
Playing the piano (controlling the movement and strength of individual fingers)	Catching and kicking a ball (timing actions, hand–eye or foot–eye co-ordination).

Note: To do these activities competently, the children need to know what to move; where to move; when to move; how to move; and, above all, how to stay safe

are functioning in the space around them. As a result, movements can hold surprises, even threaten their safety when they are nearer the kerb than they thought or when cups miss the table and clatter to the floor. They also lack planning skills – that is, the ability to know what comes first, then next – so movements can take a long time or not be attempted at all.

Some questions could cover a range of difficulties and help nursery practitioners pinpoint where the most significant ones lie – questions such as:

▶ Does the child move well, i.e. appear in control during movements, and are they confident enough to walk along a low bench? After some practice, can they do this without support? Can they ride a trike with stabilisers at 3 years old?

Such observations check the child's sense of balance and co-ordination.

▶ Can the child sit or stand still, or must they move around?

Some children need constant movement so that they have feedback as to where they are in space (see 'proprioceptive sense', Table 8.1, p. 103). This can be apparent at story time. Allowing them to sit on a beanbag, which allows some movement, can help, as does allowing them to have their backs supported against a wall. Some children can feel calmer if they are allowed to squeeze a ball of clay. Children with more severe difficulties, such as those with autism or ADHD, may flap their hands and become very agitated if they are required to be still.

Such observations check the child's sense of stability and control.

▶ Can the child crawl?

Discovering whether a child can crawl is an excellent way to check whether that child has the cross-lateral co-ordination to allow the activity to happen. Many children with additional learning needs have never crawled. Of course, there are many very clever non-crawlers too. But finding out whether a child did crawl provides one source of evidence that a specific learning difficulty might just be present.

Such observations check children's cross-lateral co-ordination.

▶ Can the child catch/kick a ball?

Observing ball skills allows a different kind of co-ordination to be checked, namely hand–eye or foot–eye co-ordination. Ball skills also show children's timing skills. Those who clutch the air after the ball has gone past may just need practice with a larger, softer ball or a balloon, preferably in a balloon bag. Adding rice can give listening clues, but they may have a tracking difficulty or be field dependent. This means that they have difficulty seeing objects as distinct from the background – rather like having no three-dimensional vision. The path of an approaching ball then would be occluded till it was too late to make the adjustments needed to catch it. Another example resulting from field dependence occurs when children can't see their slippers on a patterned carpet or find their own lunch box in a jumble of others.

Such observations check the child's hand–eye or foot–eye co-ordination, field dependence and timing skills.

77

▶ Has the child enough strength/length of limb to cope?

Children's movement can be affected by their body build. Lightly built children may avoid movement activities that may involve contact if they are nervous of being hurt. Observers have to distinguish between that and avoiding movement because of inability to carry it out.

Children with poor muscle tone (hypotonia) may also be unable to run or climb because their muscles are not providing the stability that is required. Poor muscle tone around the shoulders can prevent the arm being held firmly enough in the shoulder socket to control a pencil or paintbrush.

Such observations check how the child's movements are affected by physical/growth factors.

▶ Is the child sure which hand or foot to use – that is, the one that gives the best results?

A complete sense of hand dominance may not develop until children are 6, and in the nursery it is usual to see children use their right or left hand interchangeably. However, when they approach school age and mixed laterality continues, the children may have the linked difficulty of reversing letters and numbers. It is worthwhile speaking gently with them and asking, for example, 'Which hand did you use to do that lovely drawing?'. Or if the child is throwing a beanbag into a basket, ask, 'Which hand gets the best scores? Will we try that one again?'. This is reinforcement of what is already happening; there is no question of the children being forced to change which hand they use.

Such observations check the child's sense of hand or foot dominance.

▶ Is the child aware where the body parts are in relation to each other?

Poor body awareness is at the root of awkward, ineffective movement. Many nursery-age children aren't too sure of where their elbows, ankles or backs are. Not knowing can affect both dexterity and agility. Luckily, there are many favourite songs and jingles, such as 'Heads, Shoulders, Knees and Toes', and games, such as 'Simon Says', that provide a fun way to observe and support the children as they learn.

Such observations check the child's sense of where their body parts are and where they are in relation to one another.

▶ Can the child work at or cross the midline of the body?

Working at or crossing the midline of the body can be really difficult for some children. If a child draws a rainbow and changes the crayon over from one hand to the other at the top of the arc, this can be an indicator that this difficulty is present. As many coping skills happen at the midline, including, stirring, threading, zipping up jackets and spreading at snack time, poor competence there can be a real disadvantage. Practising figure-of-eight movements across the body (twirling ribbons can make this a fun activity) is a good way to try to help. It is also wise to try to help the children establish hand dominance.

Such observations check whether the child has a 'barrier' at the midline of the body.

▶ Is the child sure of directions and the size, shape and depth of spaces?

Spatial awareness also needs to be developed in many children who have clumsy movements. If they cannot judge the depth of a step, they are likely to fall, and mistaking the distance between two chairs, or from themselves to a friend, can lead to bumps and retaliations.

Such observations check the child's perception of the space around them.

▶ Can the child time movements? For example, in bouncing a ball, does the child contact the ball at the top of the arc, and in catching, does the arm and hand action happen at the right time or too late?

The timing of the three phases of a movement – the preparation, the action and the recovery – can determine success. If there is poor preparation, then the correct amount of strength or speed may not be gauged and the feet may not be placed in the correct position to keep the move balanced.

There are different kinds of balance. Balance is needed in a forward roll, in a jump (dynamic balance) or in a slide, or in any position that needs the body to be still (static balance) if the child is to stay in control. In the recovery phase, the body catches up with the momentum needed to carry the movement out, then slows down so that the original position is regained. From this sequence, the child should be able to use feedback so that the next try is easier. This habituation (i.e. improvement due to repetition and use of feedback) does not happen for children with dyspraxia.

It can be seen, then, that movement is complex. Children have to know what they want to do, they have to plan how this is going to happen and they have to have the physical strength and the movement abilities to carry it out.

THE LANGUAGE OF MOVEMENT

Children also need to understand directional language and some 'technical language' if they are to be able to explain their movement plans and sequences to the staff. Common terms should be part of every daily practice so that a movement vocabulary is built up. Some suggestions can form a checklist:

Run over and pass the ball	BETWEEN	the skittles
Stretch out	SIDEWAYS	to grasp the beanbag
Stand over there	OPPOSITE	me: your partner
Put your foot on the	EDGE	of the circle
Make a	ZIGZAG	pattern on the floor
Follow closely	BEHIND	your leader
Move one foot over to the	LEFT/RIGHT	and bring it back again
	CROSS OVER	to the other side
Run/walk/stroll	FORWARDS	
	BACKWARDS	
	DIAGONALLY	
	AROUND	the hoops, etc.

STAR JUMP   The arms and legs stretch out into a star shape during a jump. As some height is needed to allow time for the star to be formed, thick landing mats are needed.

BUNNY JUMP   From a crouched position, the weight goes forward on to STRONG arms. The fingers should be spread to help balance, and the arms should be positioned under the shoulders (not leaning out to the front or the side). This is a preparation for kicking horses, then handstands, so it is important to stress these basic teaching points. The eyes should look forwards to prevent a forward roll action.

TWISTING and TURNING	These two actions are different, although the words are often interchanged. TWISTING is a strong wringing action where the two sides of the body face different ways. In TURNING, the body plane faces the same way!
LEAPING	This is a description of a jump which has a single-foot take-off and aims to cover distance.
ROLLING	Rolling is an important safety movement that MUST be carefully taught. The children need to practise keeping their backs round and their elbows and knees tucked in so that only the padded bits touch the floor or the mat.

In a forward roll, the weight should be on strong arms and hands, and only the back of the head should touch the ground. Children should be shown pencil rolls as an alternative way and never be forced to forward-roll. Children with Down's syndrome should not roll forward because of instability at the top of the spine.

Before the children attempt a movement, some helpful reminders and prompts might be:

► Stand for a moment to get your balance. Are you ready?
► Tell me what you are going to do . . . first? Then after that . . . ?
► Tell me where you are going to run.
► Tell me where you have to be very careful.
► Think where the fast part comes.
► When will you slow down?
► Where will you land?

And afterwards it is useful to help the children to use feedback from the movement so that they can improve their next attempt. Use questions such as:

► How did that feel?
► How could you make it better (e.g. jump higher, run faster, take off nearer the rope – whatever is appropriate)?

81

If the child can learn to reflect and self-evaluate, this is a positive learning experience that will help the adjustment of the next attempts. It also demonstrates the usefulness of feedback and helps to ensure that the child doesn't make the same mistake over and over again. Helping children to be aware of the planning and sequencing that underlie their movements is a sure way to foster effective and efficient movement.

PRACTISING THE BASIC MOVEMENT PATTERNS

Regularly practising the basic movement patterns with lots of positive support can bring results that appear magical to the children, their families and their teachers too. Some suggestions follow.

Standing, walking and marching

Many simple walking practices are fun, can develop body awareness and can be made more interesting by using dramatic ideas – for example:

► Chocolate soldiers who march vigorously till they are too warm and melt and spread all over the floor (drooping and sinking to the floor). Jack Frost then comes along (they curl up to keep warm) but he puts icicles on their fingers and toes so they stretch right out, jump up and run off!

► Puppets/jack-in-the-boxes who walk jerkily because they are tied up with strings. They then pull the strings off from their elbows, knees, ankles and backs (body awareness practice) and dance freely all over the room till it is time to go back into their box again. This can be counted out (eight counts up and eight down again) using a tambour and beater to add to the fun and help anticipation and timing skills.

Accompanying movements with percussion or music can help the movement to be flowing and suggest changes in rhythm, speed and strength. Lines can be drawn or ropes laid out on the floor to ensure that children learn to round corners and change directions quickly without overbalancing.

Standing position

The children should be able to stand still without rocking. Feet should be reasonably close with toes pointing forward. The back of the head should be up, the shoulders low and the trunk and legs extended.

Build small-group (dramatic) activities based on walking. In these, the quality of the walk should change – for example:

1. ▶ On a cold, frosty morning walk briskly to the nursery.
   ▶ Blow out to make 'frosty breath'.
   ▶ Blow on cupped hands to warm them.
   ▶ Shake your tingling fingers (these actions help finger awareness and can also challenge balance).
   ▶ Swoop arms round to keep warm. Can you feel your hands clapping your back? (These actions help develop hand and back awareness).
   ▶ See a friend and wave. Run over to join hands and jump up and down together to keep warm.

It's fun to have a jingle to accompany the movement – for example:

Wintertime

Today it is freezing.
Just look at my nose,
It's all red and shiny.
And do you suppose
That Jack Frost has been out
and made us feel chill?
Keep jumping and shaking –
He won't make us ill!

More jingles can be found in *Jingle Time* by Christine Macintyre, published in 2003 by David Fulton Publishers (freephone 0500 618052).

2. ▶ It is very hot in the garden. You are looking everywhere trying to spot butterflies and humming birds.
   ▶ Prowl quietly through the long grass to the end of the garden. Be careful not to tramp on a beetle (slow, careful walking at a low level).

► Use big, sweeping actions to clear a path through the long grass (balance challenge).

► Curl up quietly and listen to the humming sounds (change of level and a moment of quiet).

► Notice a snake slithering through the undergrowth (raise head, straighten arms).

► Jump up and rush away – leap up into your tree house (change of speed; balance challenge in jumping and crouching).

Many stories like this can give movement practice while at the same time developing vocabulary and environmental awareness. The same kind of imaginative extensions can be applied to all the movement patterns.

ACTIVITIES TO DEVELOP FINE MOTOR SKILLS AND STRENGTHEN FINGERS

Strengthening work needs some resistance – for example, pulling through water in the swimming pool, creating roads in wet sand, moulding clay. If the children are unhappy with the texture of clay, they can often tolerate Theraputty (www.mammoetsport.nl/nldept_199.html-57k (Google search for Theraputty)).

Theraputty is a clean, malleable substance that children who dislike 'dirty clay' are usually happy to use! There are five strengths, so the density of the material can be changed as strength develops, which makes it more useful than PlayDoh, although it is more expensive. The children can pull it, mould it and stretch it. One enjoyable task is to be given a large ball of Theraputty and be asked to pull it apart to find treasure hidden inside! This involves the children in lots of pulling, which strengthens fingers, forearms and even shoulders.

Some other finger-strengthening ideas are as follows:

► Popping bubble wrap to strengthen fingers.

► Winding a yo-yo. This task asks children to have two hands doing different things at the midline of the body.

► Opening a jar of sweets and replacing them all – except one!

► Threading beads. This helps develop the pincer grip for writing.

► Picking up small objects and using them to make a collage.

► Squeezing mud, making roads in wet sand.

▶ Using a knife and fork.
▶ 'Here Is the Church, Here Is the Steeple' games.
▶ 'Incy Wincy Spider' types rhymes that have finger actions promote awareness and dexterity.

Some examples from a Primary 1 maths book show how important being able to recognise distances and directions is. Tasks such as the following can be set:

▶ Cut out the sweets and place them in the jar.
▶ Cut out the cars and put them in the car park.
▶ Draw one apple under its tree.
▶ Ring the correct number.
▶ Count on your fingers – up to ten.
▶ Lay your counters on the table (letting go is very hard).

Playing an old piano whose keys offer resistance is the best fine motor skill activity of all! The children have to concentrate on their hands (check that they are sitting in a well-balanced way), and the 'tune' gives immediate pleasing feedback.

SIMPLE FOLLOW-MY-LEADER GAMES TO HELP GROSS MOTOR SKILLS

In small groups, children enjoy marching round a room or between and round skittles following a leader.

The leader has to choose the action – for example, skipping, jogging or walking with arms swinging.

When the leader changes (and it is best to change leader often) and as the children move, the practitioner can call out, 'Leader changing to James now, everyone else in behind!'. Very often the leader chooses to keep marching. As a progression, the 'rule' can be that the action can't be the same as the one before.

Marching is the action that seems to give most enjoyment. Children who need hard feedback from the environment through the proprioceptors in their feet are free to thump, while those who have greater tactile sensitivity can do the action lightly. Each child can make a choice! The children just love being the leader, and quick changeovers mean that everyone can have a turn. In this activity, the children are learning about keeping in line. This is useful spatial training for school. It also means that they learn to tolerate being near another person and possibly being touched.

Progression

Enlarge the possible route, perhaps by giving the children the opportunity to march out of one door and back through another, which can be one way of subtly enlarging the space and changing the routine for children who find this difficult. Music or percussion can add interest as well as listening skills, and can help sort out turns.

CIRCLE ACTIVITIES

Sitting or standing in a circle (a safe, enclosing space) helps children to be aware of others sitting or standing by their side. Some children find this extremely difficult, because laterality or awareness of 'sidedness' can be slow to develop and not be fully operational till the children are 9 or so. Activities such as passing a beanbag round, or a stick with Blu-Tack or coloured tape firmly fixed to each end, soon show where difficulties lie.

Music can be used to build this into a pass-the-parcel type game.

Many old-fashioned singing games are excellent for body awareness training and developing rhythm and laterality – that is, awareness of movement at the side. Dances such as 'The Hokey-Kokey', 'In and out the Dusty Bluebells' and even 'I Sent a Letter to My Love' could supplement popular games such as 'Sandy Girl'. There are many body and spatial awareness games that ask the children go under arches or through tunnels.

If movements are carefully practised, each day they will improve, and as they form a basis for all kinds of learning, it is vital that they do. Helping children to become better movers can be great fun. Enjoy their progress. It will be so worthwhile!

Chapter 7

Understanding difficulties in paying attention and in remembering

GRAEME

Listen to Graeme, who is nearly 6. He has had an extra year in nursery to allow him to have a wider range of practical learning experiences and to allow maturation to reduce his difficulties. He tells about what it's like having a poor memory:

> When the teacher asks, 'What did we do yesterday?', he never asks me because I never remember. He says he's given up, but he always smiles and ruffles my hair, so it's not so bad. How am I to know what went on anyway? Yesterday's ages ago!'
>
> When I get home, everybody is always saying, 'What did you do at nursery today?' I remember that, because it happens every day – so I just make something up and they are always quite pleased.

Graeme is a resilient, bouncy child, as yet undismayed by his poor memory. Moreover, he not only has been able to describe his difficulty but has found the best way to cope, namely by rehearsing in his head the question he knows he will be asked, so that he is ready with an answer that will suffice! The answer, however, disguises his difficulty, so in the end is self-defeating.

His practitioner, Stuart, although pleasant and friendly, is accepting of Graeme's difficulty but not really providing any support strategies. Stuart explains:

> I know Graeme can't remember things very well, so it would be cruel to ask him to do that. I remember saying, 'Is Mum or Dad coming for you today?' and he looked blank. He knows his colours

and he has a good vocabulary – he's not stupid at all, but he never remembers, so how does he learn? I've never come across this before, so I need someone to tell me things to try.

What could those be? At the end of the day, recapping with all the children, e.g. 'Who can remember the good things we did today?', could help Graeme to hold on to what went on. Having a drawing or a photo to take home would provide a visual reminder and might allow Graeme to reply 'honestly' instead of 'just making something up' as he was doing at present. Children with poor working memories need overlearning – that is, extra repetition – so that the new learning has more chance of being retained.

Another strategy is to focus on just one activity and to explain, 'Tomorrow I'll ask you about blue and yellow. You've got to remember, OK?'. Stuart explained that Graeme liked painting and knew his colours, so he helped him mix two colours, and together they painted with the green paint (Graeme had been intrigued by the blend). As this went on, they repeated, 'Blue and yellow make green', and developed this into a jingle so that the rhythm could help too. Stuart wrote out the jingle for Graeme to take home along with his painting. He said the first three lines and Graeme added the last one. His 'homework' was to be able to remember the last line till the next day.

> Today we've made some paint – it's green,
> The nicest shade you've ever seen.
> How did we do that, do you know?
> We MIXED some blue and some yellow!

Stuart found that this had worked, and from that experience he wondered whether the nursery 'was too busy so that the day was passing in a blur'. He advised focusing on giving a child just one or two things to remember. He also stressed the importance of asking the child at the start of the day when he can remember most easily.

That will show him he can remember things when he doesn't try to remember everything and he'll get more confident. The important thing is not to overload – just to simplify what he has to remember and to give him fun ways of doing that.

Stuart was using the strategies of overlearning and rehearsal, two recognised ways of reinforcing learning. 'It was successful up to a point,' claimed Stuart, reflecting on several instances when Graeme had remembered things and had begun to volunteer without being prompted to do so, 'but it was hard for me to keep thinking of new ways to reinforce his memory; it's very difficult helping children to remember.'

KERRY

 Listen to 5-year-old Kerry, also with a poor working, memory tell about her experience:

> Mum says everything goes in one ear and out the other and that there's nothing in between – maybe she's right. I'm always in a muddle and last to get ready – like the cow's tail, she says. Everyone else laughs but I don't, for it's not funny.

Kerry's explanation shows the negative impact on confidence that having a poor short-term memory can have. Even though she seems to be accepting of this on the surface (the nursery staff spoke of her as a happy child), deep down she may come to suspect – quite erroneously – that there *is* 'nothing in between' – that she *is* stupid. Her coping strategy was 'I just go with Joanna and Kate because they know what to do and they give me a good help. They are my best friends.'

The practitioners in Kerry's nursery had visited the primary school with their children who were moving there and they had seen the buddy system working. Children from the older classes were assigned to the new children and they looked out for them in the playground and cloakroom. They also helped in a paired reading scheme – reading short stories to them in Class 1. In effect, Kerry had set up a similar scheme with Joanna and Kate. Could the school staff give the nursery any advice?

Two school members of staff, Amy and Donald, explained that their system was set up to help the younger children settle down and to ensure that no bullying went on in the playground. They considered that:

> It actually helps the older ones just as much, because by giving them responsibility for helping the little ones, we can reinforce lots of social messages. In fact, it's often the children who have been difficult themselves who respond best – it's the 'set a thief to catch a thief' syndrome all over again!

89

Asked about any misgivings, Amy and Donald pointed out that some-times the new children who wanted to show that they were 'big' felt swamped by the older ones doing too much for them and told them to go away. When that happened, the older children felt they had failed. And sometimes the older ones got fed up with giving up their break times because they were missing their football or chatting with their mates. 'We feel something like this is a short-term scheme, useful at the start of term but not for too long.'

This was useful advice, and the nursery practitioners vowed to monitor the effect on Joanna and Kate as well as Kerry. They recognised that while learning in the nursery was a co-operative venture, there could be stresses and strains within groups that they had not analysed before.

Kerry's poor memory caused her to be 'always in a muddle'. Her poor memory was influencing her planning skills. The support she needed was to be able to free her mind of all the details so that she could concentrate on one job at a time (a similar strategy to the one Stuart recommended for Graeme). The best technique for organisation and planning is to have timetables for everything possible and to use these continuously. Large ones can be made for the bedroom wall and small ones can go in a pencil case or lunch box.

Listen to Graeme's Dad, Alan, who has 'lived using timetables'. He explains:

At last it's beginning to work. We have had a real struggle to help our boy remember things, but the secret is realising that the three Rs really stand for 'routine, repetition and regularity'. The nursery told us that that we should develop as many timetables as possible and ensure Graeme learned to use them every day at the same time and in the same place.

Well, we have timetables all over the house now. What his Mum and I did was to sit down and discuss where Graeme had difficulties remembering things. We began with getting up in the morning and established a routine which included getting clothes on in the correct order [Figure 7.1]. Then we drew out a weekly timetable like a school week and marked in each day [Figure 7.2]. Each night, we moved a star along to tell him what day tomorrow was, and that saved him asking. We did one for our older boy too and we marked when his homework was given out and when PE kit had to go to school, that sort of thing. Graeme's brother is quite arty and he enjoyed drawing pictures and sticking them to his timetable. When the nursery saw we were taking this seriously, Stuart offered to have the timetables laminated, and this let Graeme see that he really wanted to know how timetables helped. Stuart also explained that if this helped him to remember, he could tell other children in the nursery and the special needs auxiliary. The downside of this promise was that Graeme wanted to do this immediately, 'in case I forget!'.

We have lists and notices all over the place. The one most used is by the front door. At first we just had a notice saying 'check your schoolbag', but found that a list of pictures, like a pencil case and lunch money, was much more helpful because it could be taken in at a glance. Once Graeme gets used to the idea, we'll try to take the timetables away and see how he copes. It's quite a simple idea, but it has helped all of us, and we really think Graeme's memory is improving. He certainly is less stressed.

The family reported that they thought that it was important for the child to be as involved as possible in making his own timetables and lists because the routine was being internalised as the charts were completed. They also advised that any children tackling this self-help strategy should be given proper materials so that they could be proud

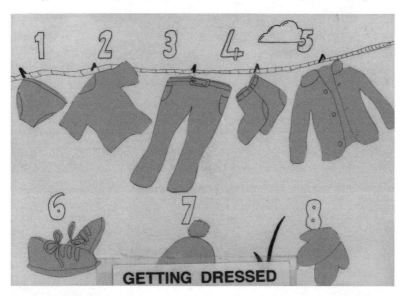

FIGURE 7.1 Picture of clothes on a line to help a child dress in the correct order

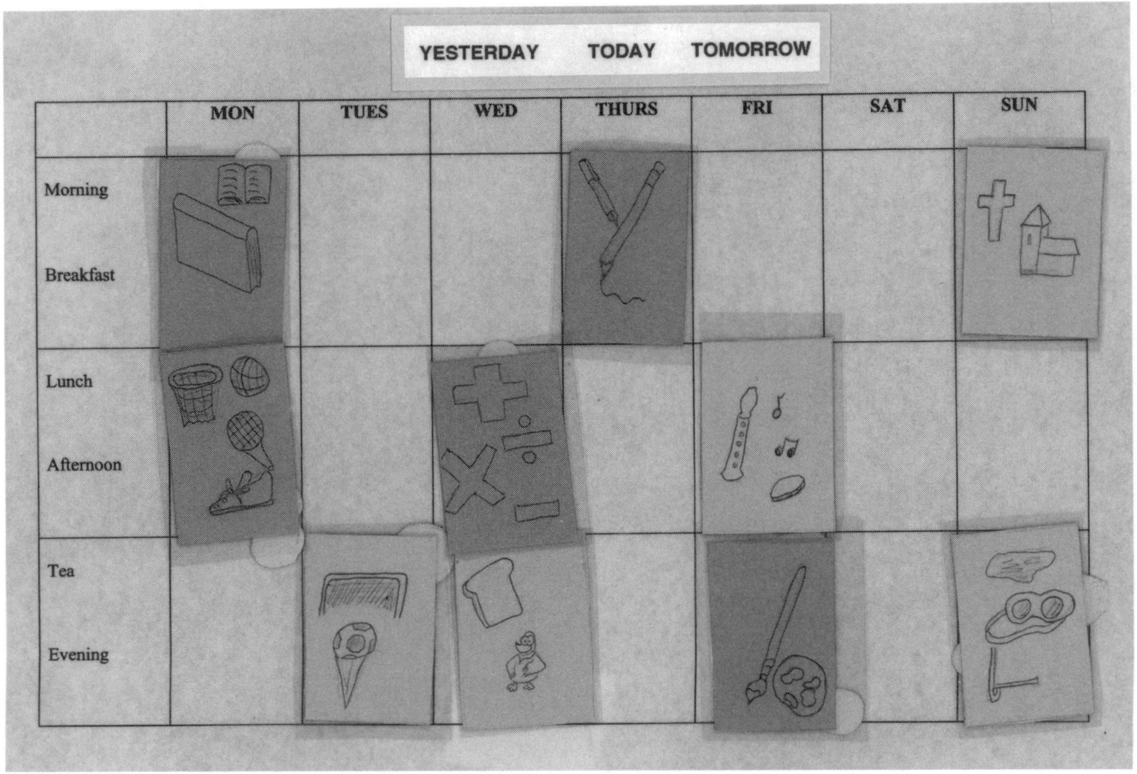

FIGURE 7.2
Timetable of the
school week

of the job and recognise its worth. Graeme's parents had found that he was able to refer to these aids and that they relieved the stress (for them) of always wondering whether he had remembered. They saw an immediate improvement in his confidence, 'as much from knowing there were strategies to help him as anything else'.

What they could not foresee was the real distress Graeme felt when an expected routine was changed.

Saying things like 'The pool is shut and we'll have to go swimming tomorrow instead of today' can throw a spanner in the works and set off a tantrum. Even a five-minute alteration in a plan is anathema to him. We had bought him a watch to help his timekeeping, but often wished we hadn't done so. He couldn't tell the time, but he could work out that when the little hand was at a certain number, a certain event was due to happen, and he became quite rigid and distressed if that didn't work. Knowing exactly when something should have happened made things worse!

So, strategies have to be tried out and sometimes they don't work. 'It's hard persevering but no one can tell till they are tried, and at the very least you are taking steps to help, not doing nothing and hoping difficulties will just go away.'

JASON

A third child, 5-year-old Jason, was perplexed and anxious, recognising both his inability to remember and the impact on his life that that was having. Listen to him explain what was wrong:

My tummy gets very sore if I've to go anywhere new because I don't know if I'll remember the way back. At home I just play around the doors and don't take my bike out much. Mum often says, 'Go and play with the other boys in the park', but they told me the wrong way to go home once so I'm not going to go with them again.

'Every day', his Mum explained, 'he asks, "Who is meeting me today?", and if I say, "Why not come home yourself?", he flies into a rage and won't go to school at all. We live very near the nursery, so we don't understand why.'

So, what is wrong and what can be done to support these children?

THE IMPACT OF A POOR SHORT-TERM (WORKING) MEMORY

The name 'short-term memory' has been replaced by 'working memory', because this term indicates the information-processing facility of the memory rather than the size or capacity of its store. A poor working memory is one feature of most of, if not all, the specific learning difficulties such as dyspraxia and dyslexia, *and* of other learning disabilities such as that associated with Down's syndrome. On the other hand, children with autism or Asperger's syndrome often have prodigious memories!

What process is involved in remembering? This is a critically important question, as without a working memory, children cannot learn. Information from the environment is received through the senses into the sensory register, where it stays for a brief time before being lost, discarded or overwritten by new information. Some of this will pass into the working memory. The amount that can be stored there will be constrained by the number of processes being carried out at the same time.

An example should clarify. If a child runs to climb up the steps of a chute at the playground in the park for the first time, then concentration is required to judge the size of step and where to place the hands to pull up on the side rails, and a further complex adjustment is needed to bring the legs through to sit at the top of the chute ready to slide down. Then attention must be paid to the gradient of the slide and the action needed to control the landing. All this complexity (the child, in deciding what to do, will also be anticipating what lies ahead and comparing that to any previous similar experiences) can prevent the child being aware of other happenings in the environment. Yet when this series of actions has been practised, the child will skim up the ladder seemingly without effort or attention and complete the sequence at the same time as hailing a friend and noticing a dog in the park and the blossom on the trees. This internalising of patterns (called habituation by Ayres (1972)) leads to efficiency in action and at the same time allows more sensory information to be noted and retained in the working memory. Many children cannot habituate. They do not seem to recognise that skills are learned patterns that can be transferred to different situations. They must learn every movement as a first-time try, and they often become very tired and frustrated as they do.

Case (1985) explains that problem-solving, which is a key learning strategy, can be impossible if the problem requires more information-

94

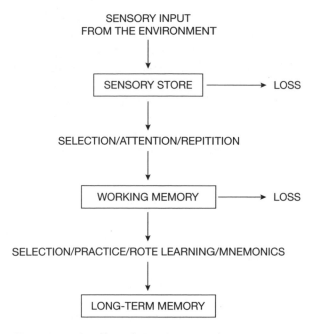

FIGURE 7.3 How the memory works

processing capacity than the child has available. This 'space' may increase with maturation, allowing more pieces of information to be stored (Kail 1990). Similarly, the processing mechanism may become more efficient, which means that fewer items need to remain in the working memory. This again leaves room for other processes to occur. These findings endorse the common-sense idea of asking children to focus on and remember just a few things at a time.

The working memory, then, is the part that holds new information and retains it for a time. Some of this information will be discarded, but if the new learning is reinforced by repetition and practice, it will pass into the long-term memory store and be available to be recalled when appropriate. When it is recalled, it goes back into the working memory until the child adapts the material to fit his or her current plan. The storage process is then repeated. If new information is not retained in the working memory, however, then repetition and reinforcement have no base on which to build, and new learning appears to 'go straight in one ear and out of the other', as Kerry described.

Children with a poor working memory may listen avidly to teaching – that is, they may be seen to pay attention – but they lose the information almost instantly. Or they may not be able to retain more than one part. Thus, some children have no recollection of previous learning, and others can retain only a snippet of what they have been told. There are children who get lost and confused because they can't remember where to go or what they are to do when they get there. There are 10-year-olds who still cannot put their clothes on in the correct order despite years of being shown, and 12-year-olds who can't remember whether they've had lunch, far less what they had to eat. There are others who cannot travel home alone, because remembering which bus to take would defeat them. Poor working memories are letting all these children down.

LONG-TERM MEMORY

The long-term memory store has unlimited capacity and can retain information indefinitely. This information can be retrieved into the working memory at will, although at times the wrong information can lead to mistakes – for example, in spelling or computation. Children with Asperger's syndrome often have a prodigious long-term memory, often surprising their parents with intricate details of events that occurred a considerable time ago. It is highly likely, however, those these are tied up with objects and events rather than personal reminiscences or the people who were there. This may also explain the Asperger's child's preference for reading factual books rather than fiction, their failure to understand someone else's pretending and their inability to relate to personal events. And so these children can be proficient in recalling information and in defining words but be less able at problem-solving. Thus, the IQ profile of children with Asperger's will have peaks (extensive vocabulary and recall of facts such as those that win TV quizzes) and troughs (comprehension, problem-solving, picture sequencing and absurdities). This explains why all aspects of children's learning must be assessed, as focusing on just one or two components can give a distorted picture, often leading to disappointment if progress (anticipated because of a wide early vocabulary) is not made.

What strategies can encourage the development of memory? The nursery advised Graeme's Dad that the three Rs were 'repetition, routine and regularity', but before these can be applied, it is essential that children pay attention.

PAYING ATTENTION

It is a truism to assert that the first consideration is to have the children pay attention to an incoming stimulus. Some have to be physically shown how to focus and how to ignore distractors in their environment. Practioners can help here by arranging for the children to work in a quiet spot away from 'buzz'. But as everyone knows, getting children to pay attention is much harder than it sounds – and this despite story and other learning episodes being stimulating and interesting, geared to the correct intellectual level of the children and being taught through varied learning experiences, including practical, hands-on activities.

Being able to identify and attend to the key features of a learning episode is a skill that develops with experience and maturity. What evidence shows this? Children of different ages shown a series of pictures, say of nine teddies dressed slightly differently, and asked to identify two the same, show very different attentional strategies (Bee 2001). The youngest ones (aged 3–6) will scan the pictures briefly and seeing two teddies with both shoes on, will immediately plump for feature and assert that these two teddies are the same. Older children (aged 6–9) will scan quickly, but then contrast and compare different elements of the picture in turn. They use much more contemplation (looking at all the teddies rather than only a few) and take time to come to a decision. They become less impulsive as they mature.

What can happen in nurseries to support children who do not go through this developmental pattern and find it difficult or impossible to pay attention?

Perhaps a signal such as a soft beat on a tambour or the sound of Indian bells can be prearranged so that the children know to focus on what is being explained. However, it may be difficult to be sure when children are and are not attending. Sometimes their body language can deceive observers, say if their gaze wanders or fixes on the floor instead of on the teacher's face. Some children can do several things at once and yet retain all the detail of what is going on. When they are asked, they can retell and give their own views. Sometimes children need to move around – for example, being allowed to sit on a beanbag – or need to squeeze a ball of plasticine as they listen or watch, because the sensory input received from these activities can help settle and overcome the urge to move around. Children with poor sensory integration (poor spatial awareness and/or a poor sense of balance) often find that such accommodations enable them to concentrate on the learning at hand.

97

Then there are children with attention deficit disorder (ADD) and attention deficit hyperactivity disorder (ADHD). Serfontein (1996) sees the names, which highlight an attention deficit, as misnomers, because children with the condition labelled ADD have a poor short-term memory, with difficulties mainly in the auditory sector. This means they have difficulty retaining spoken information even though they can be strong visual learners. There are other children who pay too much attention to particular objects. Their behaviour can be described as obsessive in cases when tiny details, not necessarily useful ones, are of paramount importance to them.

The theoretical explanations about developing strategies to help memorising, namely by rehearsal, organisation and elaboration, will now be given.

Rehearsal

'Rehearsal' is the name given to the repetition of information that happens when children need to remember something and don't write it down. Perhaps they wish to remember a jingle or a song, or they may be trying to follow a sequence of instructions such as 'Do this . . . then that . . . then go there.' Perhaps they just need to hold on to this information for a short period of time till it is recorded, or, if it is no longer useful, they choose to discard it.

Many children adopt this strategy spontaneously, but others need to have it explained to them over and over again until it is internalised and used without prompting. They need to have several – or many – demonstrations of instances when the strategy could be used, and they need sustained practice in applying it. And when an outcome dependent on the strategy has been successful, it is particularly important to take time to explain how this happened, for there is no guarantee that the children will attribute the success to the repetition – that is, the strategy that was used. This is a developmental process. Older children (aged 7+) adopt this strategy more readily than younger ones.

Organising information

Organising or grouping information into chunks is another memory aid. This can be explained to children through giving them a series of simple pictures, say of a table, a piano, a dog, a cat, a goldfish, etc., and asking them to remember as many as they can and name them a little time later. The teacher, noting the original score, can show the children how much easier it is to remember if the items are arranged into categories (in this case furniture and pets), then repeat the experiment with another set of cards. Almost certainly the score will have improved. However, this strategy is best understood after age 10 because attempts at younger ages show the children to have chosen so many categories – some containing only one item – that the organising strategy was defeated.

Elaboration

Elaboration would be useful if the children were able to imagine a series of events. Then visualisation helps memorisation. A series of items can be linked by visualising a picture that shows what comes first, then next. It seems that children remember better if the scene is humorous or ludicrous. Foley *et al.* (1993) suggested sensible and ludicrous images to young children and found that the latter group – for example, 'the black ant using a comb to fix its hair' – had the strongest retentive potential.

Again, there is a developmental/maturational aspect influencing success. While young children can be taught to use images, they have usually to be prompted to remember them. In contrast, 11-year olds are likely to conjure up an image spontaneously and enjoy using it.

The messages from researchers trialling this strategy is that many children will not use them spontaneously and need sustained coaching to do so. But in time they are helpful in retaining information in the memory – a worthwhile goal for children who find this difficult.

SYNOPSIS OF STRATEGIES TO SUPPORT CHILDREN WITH POOR WORKING MEMORIES

▶ Break down explanations and tasks into small segments and ensure that one has been retained before progressing to the next. Focus on serialistic (step-by-step) rather than holistic (giving the whole picture) input.

▶ Match the teaching input to the children's strengths. Provide visual learning whenever possible, as children with learning difficulties tend to learn best that way.

▶ Be positive and praise small items that have been remembered.

▶ Ask the children to repeat the key learning points back to you. Listen carefully to check that they have been able to do this.

▶ Take every opportunity to recap and explain how feedback from one try can be used to improve the next. Don't assume that anything will happen spontaneously.

▶ If lists or series of letters or numbers have to be memorised, teach repetition, organisation and elaboration as techniques to ease the way.

And so there are strategies to support the children, and, with the correct support, both maturation and experience can help too. But having a poor working memory is a significant disadvantage for a child, and nursery practitioners have to understand the frustration it can cause. It is a key element in several learning difficulties and impacts on all aspects of learning.

Chapter 8

Understanding difficulties with perception and sensory integration

In Chapter 2, Jack alerted us to the effect of hypersensitivity when he explained that the bright lights, loud sounds and strong smells in the nursery were upsetting him to the extent that he could not focus on his work. Other children in the same room were unperturbed, but the information Jack was taking from the environment through his eyes and nose was so acute that he was distressed. But, of course, sight, hearing and smell are just three of the senses that provide information (input) that is then processed in the brain and used to guide the subsequent action (output). In the nursery, children are often told that the senses are seeing, hearing, smelling, touching and tasting. Most enjoy feely bags (where they can't look but have to identify objects by their size and shape), and as they discriminate between one object and another, they are developing their sense of touch (the tactile sense). It is interesting to note that as they do this, the children appear to be listening intently as well, as if their auditory sense could complement their tactile one. Children who are hypersensitive to the feel of certain textures, however, will not enjoy their turn at all; in fact, they may refuse to try. Tasting sessions where the children distinguish between salty tastes, e.g. that of a savoury biscuit, and unusual sweet tastes, e.g. that of a piece of kiwi fruit, can also be tricky because now tastes are added to textures. Slightly older children may make bar charts showing the numbers of children who prefer sweet or savoury foods, and in school they will learn about where (on the tongue) these differences are identified. In this way, the early sensory learning is developed into mathematical or scientific education.

Sadly, not all children find this learning about their senses or using them straightforward, because they are hypersensitive or hyposensitive (over- or under-sensitive, respectively) to the stimuli their senses give them. They may not realise that other people do not respond to sensory input in the same way as they do, and so they may not share their difficulties and react or overreact in other ways. The nut allergy with its devastating effects is an extreme example, and nurseries are well aware of this. As a result, many do not allow food from home into the nursery now, and the contents labels on food bought in for snack time are scrutinised to make sure there are no additives and E-numbers that could cause reactions.

There are other less devastating but still important sensory influences that impact on children's learning. Some children cannot concentrate because things 'out there' distract them. They have sensory distractibility, which can be visual, tactile or auditory. So, this chapter considers all the senses – eight, not five – and gives some examples of how children's learning can be affected if any part of their sensory process does not function well enough, or too well so that they find it inhibiting or difficult or daunting or impossible to cope with the world, which at worst appears as a buzzing, booming confusion.

If they can't 'make sense' of what is going on, they may well hit out with frustration or even withdraw altogether into a safer, calmer world of their own. It is also important to remember that the different senses are used together, not in isolation, so a deficit in one can spill over to affect them all.

Let's begin by identifying all the senses and describing their key functions (see Table 8.1).

IDENTIFYING SENSORY DIFFICULTIES

Some questions follow that could indicate that there is a sensory difficulty in a nursery-age child.

Vestibular sense (indicating a poor sense of balance)

Does the child:

▶ trip a lot or fall over – seemingly over thin air?
▶ dislike leaving the ground – for example, climbing on the frame or running and jumping?

TABLE 8.1 The senses and their key functions

Sense/Key function	Effect on learning
Vestibular sense To sustain balance in a changing environment. N B. Balance is needed to give poise and control in movement. This sense is working all the time, even when the body is still.	Falls over, trips over thin air. General clumsiness: can't ride a bike or stand on one foot. Can't hop. The effort to overcome a poor vestibular sense detracts from concentration.
Auditory sense Hearing; listening. Distinguishes and discriminates between what should be heard and background noise. Cuts out unnecessary noise.	Poor discrimination hinders reading and spelling, as phonetic sounds are not differentiated. Auditory distractibility affects concentration and keeping on task.
Visual sense Seeing, tracking; identifying objects. Eyes should work together to focus and produce clear images. Children with Mears–Irlen syndrome see the letters move on the page. This hinders concentration and reading skills.	Poor functional vision may result in distorted images, affecting spatial judgements. Poor tracking results in losing the place when copying. This affects accuracy and the completing of work on time.
Tactile sense Tactile hypersensitivity results in children not being able to bear certain textures or 'dirty' hands, while hyposensitivity results in thumping to get feedback from the environment to give spatial cues.	Children are very protective of personal space and may hit out or be distressed when others come too close. Cause of anxieties and allergies.
Proprioceptive sense Gives positional information (in stillness). Proprioceptors are nerve endings found all over the skin and in the tendons and joints of the body.	If the sensations that give body position cues are latent, the child lacks body awareness, poise and dexterity, i.e. components of efficient movement.
Kinaesthetic sense Gives positional information when the body moves. Important for spatial decisions, e.g. recognising depths and distances.	A poor kinaesthetic sense results in children making poor spatial judgements, so they barge and bump. May have no intrinsic fear to keep them safe.
Senses of taste and smell Used to distinguish freshness and rancidity, e.g. in foods. Used to provide information about the environment, e.g. salty smells tell nearness to the sea. Strong smells can help judgement of distance and prevent tasting, say, disinfectant.	Gives pleasure in eating and drinking. Can prevent poisoning, e.g. drinking bleach. Can stimulate appetite (fresh bread baking!).

▶ seem reluctant to go outside (which may mean bumpy grass or uneven paths)?

▶ squirm around at story time?

▶ flap hands or wriggle, finding it difficult to be still?

▶ become tired or floppy through using energy to stay balanced?

Auditory sense (indicating under- or over-sensitivity in hearing)

Does the child:

▶ fail to screen out extraneous noises and so become distracted or distressed by sounds?

▶ become overly distressed by noises that sound 'normal' to others?

▶ have to make a noise, e.g. thump around, to gain spatial feedback?

▶ seem in a world of their own, not responding to movements around them?

▶ fail to react to other people calling?

▶ have difficulty distinguishing between different sounds?

▶ have an articulation difficulty?

(An auditory processing difficulty might be helped by a Listening Program. See www.advancedbrain.com for information.)

Visual sense (indicating poor sight or poor functional vision)

Does the child:

▶ have difficulty focusing on a picture in a book?

▶ rub his or her eyes or shake the head as if trying to clear vision?

▶ find threading beads very difficult?

▶ find bright lights disturbing?

▶ miss or misinterpret non-verbal cues?

▶ have difficulty catching a sympathetically thrown large, soft ball?

Communication

▶ Can the child hold eye contact?

▶ Does the child use eye/facial/postural expressions to communicate meaning, or avoid looking at the speaker?

Tactile sense

Does the child:

▶ hate being touched?

▶ like to touch others?

▶ over-protect his or her personal space?

▶ become irritated by seams in clothes?

▶ hate having his or her hair and nails cut?

▶ have an over- or under-sensitive reaction to pain?

▶ need tactile reassurance, e.g. regular tight hugs?

▶ want to be swaddled in an anorak or thick jumper?

▶ complain of being too hot or cold when others are fine?

Proprioceptive sense

Does the child:

▶ seem restless and inattentive?

▶ have arms and legs 'all over the place'?

▶ take a long time to get up and go?

▶ make wispy drawings because of poor judgement of strength required?

▶ seem tense and afraid of what might happen?

Kinaesthetic sense

Does the child:

▶ get lost, even within the nursery – for example, can't find the toilets?

▶ have poor body awareness when moving, knocking into tables and chairs?

▶ not sense obstacles in his or her path?

> ► make poor depth perception decisions – for example, will jump into deep water or off a wall that is too high for safety?

Senses of taste and smell

Does the child:

> ► become distressed by new scents and smells?
> ► refuse to taste new foods?
> ► only tolerate a restricted diet?
> ► want to drink or eat unsuitable items, e.g. pieces of wood from the woodwork table?
> ► complain that friends or places smell bad?

DEALING WITH SENSORY DIFFICULTIES

Just one or two difficulties might ease with maturation and experience, but a check should be kept in case difficulties persist. If there are several 'yes' responses, help should be sought, as additional learning needs *may* be indicated, and even if this proves not to be the case, steps can be put in place to help children overcome their specific difficulties. Sensory integration therapy provides gentle experiences, such as sitting on a rocking horse then allowing it to be gently rocked, or lying on a trampoline, just feeling the sensation, then tolerating a gentle bounce. (This is rebound therapy, and training courses are available. It is used to give pleasurable sensations to profoundly disabled children, but many others can enjoy it and benefit too.)

HOW DOES SENSORY PERCEPTION WORK?

The different senses work together to act as receptors of information from the environment in what is called sensory integration (Ayres 1972) or cross-modal transfer (Bee 2001). The information passes to the brain for analysis and then the efferent system instructs the muscle groups how to respond. Goddard (2002) describes this process when she writes:

> All learning takes place in the brain, but it is the body which acts as the vehicle by which knowledge is acquired. Both brain and body work together through the central nervous system but both are dependent on the senses for all information about the outside world.

This quotation emphasises the importance of sensory input to movement and learning and coping with all the activities of daily living.

SENSORY DECISION-MAKING IN THE NURSERY

Think of nursery children coming into the nursery and deciding where to play. How do their senses contribute to their choice? First, their vision will let them know the kinds of activities that are on offer. Some will choose the most colourful and lively ones, while that same brightness will deter others. They will also use their vision to make decisions about where they are allowed to go, remembering the nursery rules – for example, that only four can use the water or sand trays at once. The visual picture will provide clues rather than depending on the children counting out the bodies! Their sense of smell will possibly tempt them to investigate what is cooking for snack time, and at the same time it will provide clues as to how long they have to wait before they can taste, for biscuits and cakes 'smell ready', do they not? So, the sense of smell can be linked to timing decisions – for example, 'Will I sit and wait or go to painting for a short spell first?'.

Imagine, then, that the children decide to sit at the table ready for their snack. Those who make good spatial decisions will not have to look to check where the seat is, because their proprioceptors tell them how far they have to bend. Those who have faulty input will bump and barge and knock into each other, and the plates will land on the floor. The bumping and clattering can offend children with auditory sensitivity, so the clumsy ones will be faulted for that as well. The children's kinaesthetic sense tells them if they are near enough the table or whether they have to adjust their position. The vestibular sense is working hard to keep the children balanced as they sit. It has to work overtime if the children rock in their seats or fidget or keep moving when they should be still. Then the sense of taste is employed, along with the sense of smell to decide whether the snack is to their liking. A hyperactive tactile sense can prevent some children handling things with rough textures, such as oatcakes, while an under-active sense means that spreading is very difficult, especially if there is a 'crossing the midline' difficulty.

All activities can be broken down like this, and such an analysis can pinpoint specific difficulties and guide decisions about intervention – that is, the kind of support strategies that should be put in place.

In nursery, the children can make many choices, and they may, without knowing it, be adapting to their sensory preferences. But in

107

school the children are told where to sit and have to stay there for set periods of time. Their situation, such as being near a window or a humming radiator, may cause their auditory and visual distractibility to be activated. This means that in concentrating to overcome these urges (to see and listen to all the movement and bustle of children passing the window, perhaps), they are distracted from focusing on the lesson that is being taught. In addition, if their table or desk is not at the correct height, their balance is jeopardised, and this is made worse if their chair has spindly metal legs that invite rocking and overbalancing. In preparing their seating plan according to social or ability concerns, practitioners may forget or not realise that sensory implications should be considered too.

The senses can also trigger memories that can complement or detract from learning. A hot smell from the nursery cooker can remind children of an event – perhaps when they had popcorn at the fair – and thereby stimulate their memories and their vocabulary, and make a conversation much more interesting. Alternatively, that same smell can really upset a child who remembers a frightening house fire or a bonfire out of control. Practitioners, not recognising the source of the dismay or even the tears or anger, could think the child's reaction was unreasonable.

These are the more obvious outcomes from sensory input. There is, however, a more subtle one that underlies confidence and how children approach new learning tasks.

DEVELOPING A SENSE OF SELF: THE SELF-CONCEPT

Through their senses, children develop a sense of self – that is, they come to realise they are separate beings detached from anything else and that they have the power to make things happen. Children need this sense of identity to allow them to develop security and confidence, even to develop their imaginations. This is quite subtle, but how could children know how someone else was feeling if they did not understand that they themselves have hopes and fears and that certain things make them happy or sad?

Relationships are built on this basis of understanding. The definition of how the self-concept is formed is complex. It is a tri-dimensional image, formed in the process of growing up. This means that a child's sense of self (what they are, where they are and why they are there) is a part of the developmental process, and in the early years especially it fluctuates, depending largely on how the child is affected by the responses of those closest to them. Psychological literature would call these people 'significant others'. The fluctuation also involves changes in the importance of these people. In the earliest years, parents and close relatives form this group. Bonding with them is extremely important, because this relationship provides security before the child has the skills to be independent. Then the practitioners in school take over the 'significant other' role for a while. Parents can be very upset when their ideas are rejected in favour of what 'Miss So and So says'. Hopefully, adults accept this as part of the child's growing up process and, despite feelings of rejection, retain their love and support for their child. Later, the dependency on the practitioners becomes redundant and the peer group become the most important influence in a child's life. These people are all providing models for behaviour, dress, or whether to learn in school or not. After a time of uncertainty, the cycle comes round, and the earliest relationships become the most significant again. It is to be hoped that children will pass through this turbulent process with positive input from all the significant others, so that their confidence stays high. Perhaps the uncertainty contributes to the strong desire to be the same as those they admire.

As this process goes on, the children begin to reflect on and evaluate the competences they have. Children with additional learning needs come to realise that they are different, and that hurts. It is critically important that all their significant others support them so that they too can have a positive self-concept. While these children are more subject to disappointments and frustrations as they come to recognise that they are different, the people important to them have to show that they recognise and applaud the qualities they do have and share with them ways to help reduce the effect of their difficulties. They have to be accepted and valued for what they are, not made to feel inadequate in an increasingly competitive world.

Self-esteem

The evaluation part of the self-concept is called self-esteem. If it becomes low – and it does if children believe they fall short of the picture they have of their ideal self – it can be very difficult to give it a boost. This is why giving realistic but positive feedback to each child must be every practitioner's goal.

In the early years, children are tied to that picture. They are egocentric. They see the world in relation to themselves. This is because they have not developed the awareness or had the experiences to allow them to look beyond their small world, to make comparisons and to learn how to associate with others. But gradually they do become sociocentric and develop empathy and altruism – that is, understanding how others feel, celebrating with them when things go well and caring for them when things go awry. Children with autism and Asperger's syndrome do not develop this empathy, as they do not appreciate the feelings others have and so they do not understand how their comments or actions can hurt others. With no intention to wound, they will ask, 'Why are you fat?' or 'Why have you got nasty clothes?'. In the light of this, it is easier to understand children who comment inappropriately about their peers and show no remorse when they are obviously upset.

However, most children will be aware of how others are looking and feeling and even thinking, and gradually they begin to make comparisons between themselves and others. It is not surprising that many of those with additional needs feel vulnerable, and this leads them to becoming increasingly intractable or withdrawn and fearful of facing the world.

The way adults interact is crucial. There is no point in telling children that they do not have a problem when they are perfectly aware one exists. That only destroys trust. The best way forward is to accept a difficulty (keeping it in proportion), but at the same time, plan and share a programme that will help the children to overcome it, or at least reduce its effects.

Another tried and tested strategy is for a practitioner and a child to compile a 'things I am good at' list. This can follow naturally from praise: 'What a good boy to tidy away your snack dishes. I wonder what other things you do well? Can you help me to make a list to show Mum?'

An experienced practitioner, Anthea, tried out this strategy with Ruth, who was very timid. At first, Ruth looked alarmed and the staff thought it best to wait, but the next day she volunteered, 'I'm goodest at dancing'. And that heralded the start of the list. A ballet corner was set up in the nursery, and that gave other ideas. Percussion was added (the tambourine with flowing ribbons was a huge success), and the children soon learned to handle a tape with care and work the tape recorder. The sequence for this was put up as a laminated list of picture instructions, numbered 1, 2, 3. Warmed by her success in the dancing corner and prompted by the staff, Ruth was able to agree that she was good at other activities across the nursery.

Ruth's list: I am good at

Dancing
Putting the tape on
Twirling in front of the mirror
Eating fruit at snack
Finding my name
Helping Tom to finish his jig-saw.

The list began to grow when Ruth realised that small items were important. Gradually she gained in confidence. Of course, no one could claim that the list alone was responsible, but it gave a focus for communication with Anthea, who found it 'a good way to get to know a child'. Later, when Ruth was able to confide that 'I'm not very good at catching a ball', Anthea was able to ask, 'Would you like a little bit of help?'. In this way, a teaching episode developed from the idea of making a list.

Vulnerability and bullying

It is a very sad fact that vulnerable children, often those with additional learning needs and/or low self-esteem, can be the target for bullies. Is this the case in nurseries? Can grabbing toys and pushing other children really be called bullying? Is 'not getting to play' on a regular basis being bullied? Although this may seem trite in comparison to other aspects of behaviour, occurrences like this can spoil a child's day and have a marked negative effect on self-esteem, even stopping the child from wanting to come to nursery at all. Yet it is not easy to help that child to get into a game.

If the offending children claim they were 'just larking around', but caused hurt, what then? In the nursery, the higher staff:pupil ratio and the constant observation can avert bullying and aggressive behaviours, but children who might become bullies have to be identified and helped to overcome this tendency for their own sakes as well as for their victims' well-being. They must recognise the effect of their actions. This may sound obvious, but spotting bullies can be difficult, as even at 4 years old they learn to hide their actions and their taunts. Furthermore, the ones who thought up the dire deeds may not be the ones who carry them out. In fact, vulnerable children can be pulled into the bullying group as they seek for ways to appease or to join the bullying band. They are seeking to protect themselves, but could be mistaken for being bullies themselves.

Rather than naming and shaming, a first intervention could be to use puppets (e.g. an angry toad, a bullying bat, a timid tortoise, a miserable mole) and build a story in which one of the animals is a bully and another is unhappy because of that. In that way, the children can learn to empathise with the one who was distressed by the actions of the others. Unfortunately, verbal agreement that a certain behaviour is unacceptable or hurtful doesn't mean that the perpetrators will necessarily change their ways, but reminders – 'Remember poor Mole?' – can then be used to show individuals that their behaviour has been noted and disapproved, without using the much more emotive language of bullying at all.

Different kinds of bullying

Physical hurt

Physical hurt can vary from nudging to actual bodily harm. It is the uncertainty, the 'not knowing when it is going to happen', that can destroy confidence as much as the actual hurt. The damage may be done to the victim's property or work rather than to the person, but this can be just as devastating. Children who appreciate that their families will find it difficult to replace things that have been spoiled, or children who have made a huge effort to produce lovely work to take home, can become very distressed.

Verbal abuse

Verbal abuse too can be on a continuum, in this case from teasing to taunting to using sarcasm to wound. Bullies can always find something, whether it is a child's size or shape or ethnic background, or just not being able to do something the others can. When the recipient shows hurt and vulnerability, the bullies know they have won. This is why bullying must be stamped out rather than hoping it will go away.

There are various theories about why children bully. Some see the bully as a vulnerable youngster who is using this strategy to overcome problems. Another group deny this, saying that bullies are very aware of the effect they are having. Despite many policies and conferences that aim to find a solution, bullying still goes on. What a wonderful contribution the nursery could make to lifelong education if anti-bullying seeds were seen to thrive.

Chapter 9

Understanding behaviour difficulties

Listen to nursery staff talk about their experiences in coping with children who are disruptive and find it difficult to settle into the nursery routine. Laura, an experienced practitioner, begins:

> More and more children who can't or just won't conform to our ways of working are coming into nursery now. It used to be that we had an occasional child who didn't know how to behave, and with patience and tolerance he would settle down. Having one child like this meant that one practitioner could be assigned to watch and step in if things got out of hand. Also, the school management team would help us to get professional support, because that child was so different to the norm. But now we have a whole group of children who upset the apple cart on a daily basis, so *they* have become the norm, and no one wants to know. So what do we do? Just watch until all our years of work is destroyed?

Unfortunately, others endorsed this sad story. After just two years, Daniel was on the point of leaving nursery education altogether. He explains:

> People just don't believe that nursery children can be worse than naughty; they just look at me as if I must be crazy not to be able to control 4-year-olds. I can understand children being badly behaved if they have learning difficulties, or that they need time to adjust to the nursery ways of working, because some children have such terrible lives at home. But we have a continual battle to get them to behave, and their parents don't support us. I'm not paid to put up with their cheek at best, biting and spitting at worst. It seems

that no one can tell us what to do – at least, not anything that works. Our headteacher tells us that 'some of these children will behave badly all the way through school'. We know what to expect, but when we mention exclusion, the shutters come down. They are building up problems for themselves, because when they get bigger and stronger, these kids will be totally out of control.

Laura and Daniel have painted pictures of conflict that are hard to resolve. There is no magic wand to make children behave. But why should such young children sustain, even relish, conflict? Strategies to address this difficult issue must be grounded in the knowledge of the children's life experiences – that is, their home environment and the kinds of 'rules' if any, that they follow there – as well as their genetic make-up – that is, their temperament, or any difficulties such as ADHD that are not their fault. Behaviour difficulties rarely occur in isolation. Any co-occurring difficulty must not be overlooked, and practitioners must ensure that the children really understand what is expected of them in a complex and very different environment.

Then practitioners must reflect on their own reactions to children and discover whether they are inadvertently 'fanning the flames'. Some general but very valuable pointers for communication have been written for children with ADHD, but could equally benefit children with other learning or behavioural needs. These descriptors come under the heading of 'reframing' and are ways of changing how the children's characteristics are described (see Table 9.1). The question of whether and to what extent changing words can change attitudes is a fascinating one.

Conflict of any kind is uncomfortable to live with. How can practitioners not resent the source of disruption – that is, the children who just won't conform to the accepted ways of behaving in nursery? And is that tension communicated to the children, who sense some kind of stress or 'false welcome' whenever they arrive? Harris (1992) points out that 'children with special needs fit into a group that are accepted'. This is good. But he goes on to show that 'badly behaved children are not regarded sympathetically. Everyone recognises that any bad behaviour has a just cause – but badly behaved children with no recognised syndrome are resented because they are seen to spoil the learning environment for everyone else'. Poor behaviour is not always seen as an additional learning need. It seems that some other parents and some exhausted practitioners would rather these children go somewhere else, even anywhere else.

115

TABLE 9.1 'Reframing' of children's negative characteristics

Negative comments	Reframing
Being out of seat too much	Energetic and lively
Talking out of turn or calling out	Keen to contribute
Losing and forgetting things	Thoughtful; absorbed in own ideas
Distractible	Has a high level of environmental awareness
Impatient	Goal oriented
Has difficulty converting concepts into words	A visual, concrete thinker
Daydreams	Is bored by mundane tasks. Imaginative

Source: G. Craig, *A Guide to Intervention and management of pupils with ADHD*. Edinburgh: North-West Edinburgh ADHD-Pilot Project

Within any community there are different standards of behaviour. By the time children are 4, they have internalised the behaviour of their early role models. These are their parents, their siblings and their television 'heroes', who can be even more aggressive and bullying than those they meet at home. When these children come to nursery, they have to adapt to a totally different culture in which shouting and aggression are not the normal way of interacting. This is not an easy transition, and children can feel lost or can resent the unspoken implication that nursery ways are 'better' than home ways. Even at home, some children are fighting to survive. They have to jettison what may be a naturally reticent temperament and become loud to demonstrate that they can do as their siblings do, especially if the parents approve of the way these older children behave. As Harris (1992) explains, 'cultures teach children to express certain emotions and suppress others'. When the expectations of home and school 'match', the child is eased into a new situation, but when they are very different, the child has to make a cultural shift that can be confusing and hard to sustain.

But of course this is only one scenario, and many others exist. There are model parents bewildered by their child's behaviour, because their other children behave well. Others pamper their children to the extent that learning to share toys or attention with others at the nursery becomes a major hurdle. Some simply don't understand why their children behave as they do. They do their best to 'make their children behave', but despite their efforts, 'nothing works'. This may be devastating for them, and, especially if this is an only child, they blame their parenting skills and often feel too vulnerable to share their anxieties with the nursery. On the other hand, some can endorse their child's behaviour and resent any implication that there are other, better ways to behave.

But to believe that 'nothing will work' is a no-win situation for parents, practitioners and, worst of all, for the children themselves. So, what can be done?

Louise, who has been a key worker in an inner-city nursery, gives her advice.

> Somehow a relationship between the school and the home *has* to be established so that all the adults can work together to support the child. If not, the parents blame the nursery and the nursery blames the parents, and the children in the middle are either bewildered or they learn to play one off against the other. Yes, even at 4, they know exactly how to do this! Home visits can help if the parents are willing to talk to us, but often they don't want to cross the boundaries. Sometimes they have other problems to deal with, and a child not behaving at nursery takes low priority.

Certainly, any meeting has to happen on equal terms. Parents don't want to have advice or hear sentences that begin 'You should do . . .'! Both parties can start off feeling vulnerable but easily become resentful. The trouble is that even if both are willing to meet and discuss, any change takes time, and meanwhile the child can become 'increasingly entrenched in their pattern of responding' (McLean and Brown 1992), making change all the harder to achieve.

When building relationships proves difficult, what other strategies can be tried? 'Our nursery team has a list of strategies,' claimed Vicky, 'and when we have a child with behaviour difficulties we try to adhere to these. Later we try to reflect honestly to see if we've managed to hold on or not!'. She was willing to share her list.

First of all, check for additional learning needs. Then find out about the child's background and see whether clues lie there. Once these checks have been made, the next steps are as follows:

▶ Make sure the nursery layout helps: arrange tables so that there is no long passageway to encourage charging around; replace the woodwork bench with clay; check all safety factors – for example, take down the climbing frame. Arrange a chill-out section in the room and have music playing softly in the background.

▶ Give the child the same welcome as the others. Look positive but don't be overwhelming. Avoid making reference to behaviour, such as 'I hope you are going to be good today'. Try to convey the expectations that the child will be good!

▶ Speak and move around quietly. Act as a role model for how you would like the children to behave.

▶ Look for instances where the child has merited praise and give immediate positive feedback. Catch them being good. Even doing something quietly can be praised. Note what kind of praise the child enjoys. Some like the other children to know they have done well; others prefer a quiet word or just a smile and a nod.

▶ Observe the child carefully and try to anticipate any swing in mood that might suggest they are about to erupt. Try to distract them by suggesting another activity.

▶ If the child is engrossed, don't interrupt to ask if they have had their snack. Try to time interventions so that they don't cause conflict.

▶ Avoid asking questions to which the child can answer 'No', such as 'Would you like to do . . . ?' Rather, say, 'Time for story now; come over to the carpet. Thank you for doing this quickly'.

▶ Give warning of any changes, such as 'It's nearly time for . . . Can you finish off quite soon so that you are ready?'.

▶ Observe from a distance rather than swamping the child. Try not to make them feel different from the others.

▶ If all else fails, have the child sit on a beanbag to chill out for a short time. Give them an egg timer so that they can see how long they have to stay there. Once the child is there, don't give them any attention. Even if the child is shouting and swearing, try to ignore him. When the time is up, immediately re-establish a positive relationship.

▶ If the child tries to harm another, he or she must be restrained. Call for assistance.

Dean considered that a different approach suited him best. He explained:

I don't think you can expect children to come into nursery and not give vent to their feelings. When Kev comes in looking upset, I say something like 'Had a bad day, Kev? Me too! Want to tell me about it?'. Sometimes he grins and runs off and that's great. We've established that I am there for him. If he says 'No', then I don't press him, but he knows no matter what, I'm on his side. If he's really upset, I'll say, 'What about playing the guitar for a while?'. Then he cheers up. He thinks that's cool and he'll ask me to play tunes or try to play it himself. He tells me he wants to play at T in the Park one day, so this is a good activity for him. He's always calmer after that.

Dean had found a tactic that worked for Kev, but this involved him in a one-to-one arrangement that is not always possible. In general, is this a good idea, or in this instance was success due to Dean's personality, his ability to empathise and his skill in playing the guitar?

After special needs (including behavioural needs) auxiliaries came into nurseries and schools, there were mixed evaluations concerning one-to-one situations. While no one denied that 'it was wonderful to have someone responsible for a particular child', sometimes this provision was regarded as the total commitment to 'inclusion', and was inadequate. Some auxiliaries resented the fact that they 'had to cope with no training'. They claimed that in some nurseries, 'the practitioners just let us get on with trying to cope with the difficult children and we don't really know what to do'. Moreover, they came to realise that their constant presence was stopping the other children playing with their child and preventing that child trying to make friends. Later they realised that some of their special children were becoming deskilled. They were waiting for the auxiliary to do things they could perfectly well do for themselves. Often the auxiliary was taking over because no one had set out the parameters of her role. 'What was I to do?', asked Irene. 'I had to be seen to work if I wanted to keep my job.'

McLean and Brown (1992) pointed out another downside of having one-to-one help for children with behaviour difficulties. They claimed that 'providing support may inadvertently reinforce the children's self-image as disruptive people who need a practitioner to themselves. Some enjoy the notoriety, some are embarrassed and others become annoyed

119

by the presence of the supporter and refuse to co-operate'. They also pointed out that if this refusal occurs, 'it should be seen as just that, not as further evidence of emotional disturbance'. And so there are pros and cons that have to be carefully thought through in the light of individual children's preferences and reactions, and in the wisdom of experience. Understanding this can prevent adults considering they have failed the child.

'Emotional disturbance' is an emotive term, yet it does describe the traumas many young children endure. Can understanding the development of emotions help nursery practitioners to devise strategies to support children who find conforming to set routines difficult?

Children are often encouraged to keep their emotions in check, particularly when interacting with younger children. Understanding how *they* feel is taken as a sign of maturity. 'When a quarrel breaks out, the instigator is expected to apologise and the injured party is expected to accept this and not seek further retribution' (Harris 1992). As children come to appreciate this, they are learning display rules, as when a child has to politely thank an adult for something the child really doesn't want! But of course not all children have this kind of experience, and so when they arrive at nursery they are less well attuned to expressing their own feelings or appreciating that their actions directly impinge on the feelings of others.

Bee (2001), however, points out that by 4 years, children should be developing altruism, and she claims that even if this is delayed, 'children have the cognition to understand the relationship between actions and outcomes'. To test this, she prepared a short imaginary scene and asked children of different ages for their response. The story they were told was as follows:

You are on your way to a party when you see a boy who has fallen over and hurt his foot. He can't walk and is crying. What would you do?

Four-year-old: 'Is there ice cream at the party? What games will we play?'

Five-year-old: 'I'd phone his mother on his mobile before I went to the party.'

Six-year-old: 'I'd put him on my back and we'd both go to the party. The jelly will make him feel better.'

Ten-year-old: 'I'd wait with him till help came and make sure his mum knew where he was.'

The developmental change is evident in these replies. The youngest child latched on to the word 'party' and was not going to be delayed. The next was more responsible, but after making a call, he too was off. The third child was more considerate of the boy and reckoned a change of scene would help. But this tactic meant he didn't miss the party either. The last was clear what the most acceptable response was – but rather spoiled it by the add-on, 'I don't like parties anyway!'

Harris (1992) develops this theme, explaining that by the age of 6, children have the intellectual capacity to know they can alter situations and so change their emotions. Harris offers the following exchange with a 4-year-old as an example:

Interviewer: Say you were ill and felt sad, is there anything you could do to change the way you felt? To get rid of the feeling of sadness?

Child: I'd try to be happy.

Interviewer: How?

Child: By playing about and thinking about a happy day.

These interviews were carried out with 5-, 6-, 7-, 8-, 9- and 10-year-olds, and all of them identified some change of activity 'to distract me from the sad situation' (10-year-old boy's response).

Could this strategy help in the nursery? Dean tried it out. He described his attempt:

Kev had gone haywire and knocked Emily into the easel, spilling water over her dress and tearing her painting. He wouldn't say he was sorry, so had to sit on the beanbag to chill out. I tried to follow Harris's pattern.

Dean: Are you feeling a bit sad?

Kev: No – well maybe a wee bit sad.

Dean: Could you change things so you were happy again? (He had been good all morning till that episode when he was out of control.)

Kev: Nobody cared that I got a fright, did they? (He was rocking back and forwards.) But I will say sorry if I get to play with the train set. I'll be happy then!

Dean was slightly taken aback, but Kev did say sorry, and the nursery practitioners, ignoring the last comment, thought it had been a reasonably positive exchange. They thought the strategy was worth repeating because the child was left in charge of deciding on a solution rather than their telling him what he had to do. They described this as a 'recipe for confrontation'. They were also aware that Kev was justified in claiming that no one had comforted him!

Most, if not all, children with behaviour difficulties have low self-esteem. It is not easy to give it a boost. They have to learn that people are willing to admire and respect them. Even very young children can make this hard. But children have their own strategies for coping too, and one strategy can be to deny or cease to think about any emotionally charged event. Bringing it back to their conscious level through recriminations may not be the most helpful thing to do. Each day has to be a fresh start. Consistent, quiet routines in which expectations are made explicit are usually the best way to help children settle.

There are no quick ways to change children's behaviour, but surely listening to them explain their perceptions, their fears and the things that make them happy is a start. Then, acting on these confidences may mean considering different approaches.

In the light of the research that brought about this book, no one can doubt that very young children can tell about their fears, their hopes and their dreams . . . if only someone will take time to listen to what they have to say.

Part III

Overview

Chapter 10

Overview of conditions for which children need additional support

There are many detailed texts that give a comprehensive account of each special needs condition. It is beyond the scope of this one to compete. This chapter gives a brief account and gives a list of places where further help may be sought. Diagnosis is a complex undertaking, and nursery practitioners should be careful not to imply to parents that a special needs condition is present.

Before this overview begins, it is necessary to recap on key points that have been visited in the previous chapters.

▶ The difficulties that have been identified in these nursery children may indicate that one or more of the following conditions may be looming. However, they may be overtaken by maturation and experience, as well as the support the children receive at nursery and at home. Early intervention does not mean that a label must stick.

▶ Although there are specific indicators for most, there is a great deal of overlap across conditions. This sometimes causes confusion in making a diagnosis, especially if the child's performance fluctuates from day to day and between environments. It is very difficult to find the 'pure' child.

▶ In making assessments, all facets of the child's ability should be considered. In specific learning difficulties, there is a dip in one aspect of development. In children with comprehension difficulties, a wide vocabulary may hide the fact that they do not understand the meaning of what is being said. Focusing on one blip in isolation would give a distorted picture of the child's development.

► Many children with additional learning needs look just the same as other children and learn to disguise their difficulties. They have a hidden handicap, so close observation is the key to supporting them.

► The effects of giving a label and the timing of suggesting that one is required are issues that must be considered sensitively. Each region has a policy for seeking specialist support. It is essential that these procedures are followed.

► Gaining the consent of the parents is mandatory before any contact with outside agencies is made.

IDENTIFYING THE OVERLAP

The overlap of some key difficulties is shown in Table 10.1.

TABLE 10.1 Overlap of key difficulties

	Movement	Memory	Literacy/ mathematics	Communication	Planning and organisation
Dyslexia	*	*	*		*
Dyspraxia	*	*			*
ADD		*			*
ADHD	*	*			*
Down's syndrome	*		*	*	*
Asperger's syndrome	*	*		*	
Autism	*	*		*	*
Behaviour difficulties		*		*	*

Note: ADD, attention deficit disorder; ADHD, attention deficit hyperactivity disorder

In Canada, Kaplan *et al.* (2001) claim that 'Co-morbidity [overlap or co-occurrence are the more common terms used in Britain] is the rule rather than the exception'. They use the term developmental co-ordination disorder (DCD) in place of dyspraxia. Their statistics show that:

▶ 33 per cent of those with attention deficit hyperactivity disorder (ADHD) also have DCD;

▶ 52 per cent of those with dyslexia also have DCD.

In London, Keen (2001), a paediatric consultant, has also researched this overlap. She reports that:

▶ 30 per cent of children with learning difficulties also have ADHD;

▶ 30–40 per cent of children with ADHD also have learning difficulties;

▶ 50 per cent of children with ADHD have dyspraxia;

▶ 50 per cent of children with dyslexia also have dyspraxia;

▶ 8 per cent of children with autism also have Tourette's syndrome.

In identifying the shared areas of dysfunction, she sees them as:

▶ a discrepant cognitive profile;

▶ difficulties in sequencing and ordering;

▶ impairments of social understanding;

▶ executive function deficits (short-term memory, focus, adaptation to change).

These findings show how important it is that observers and assessors do not latch on to the first indicators, or misdiagnoses are sure to result. Communication with parents is a must, because they can confirm or deny observations. They can also share instances of the same behaviours happening at home or explain any change at home that may contribute to changed behaviours.

We shall now consider a number of named difficulties.

ATTENTION DEFICIT HYPERACTIVITY DISORDER (ADHD)

ADHD is a complex neurobiological disorder. The chemical messengers in the brain, such as dopamine, may be deficient, and some parts of the brain may be smaller than usual. This leads to difficulties with paying attention, concentrating, taking time to consider the effects of actions (i.e. impulsivity) and in some cases hyperactivity. This is a medical condition. Children are slow to learn self-management skills and so take longer to become independent. This is not due to laziness or bad behaviour.

Five per cent of children are affected worldwide (Learning Assessment and Neurocare Centre, www.lanc.uk.com).

▶ There are two kinds of attention deficit disorders. The first has inattention as a key indicator while the second houses impulsivity and hyperactivity as well.

▶ The boy:girl ratio is 5:1. Boys tend to be aggressive; girls more often have inattention as the main difficulty. This may lead to the condition not being properly diagnosed.

▶ Symptoms can be mild, moderate, severe or fluctuating. They may be combined with other conditions. Two-thirds of children will have another difficulty such as dyspraxia, dyslexia or oppositional defiant disorder.

▶ The condition, because it affects concentration, impacts on progress in learning. Frustration can take over, or triggers can cause uncontrollable reactions in severe cases.

▶ After detailed assessments, medication may be recommended. Close monitoring is needed to ensure that the child takes the medication and that it has no untoward effects.

▶ Around 90 per cent of children with ADHD can show significant progress as they mature, but delay in obtaining professional support will only lead to problems with self-esteem and all the negative connotations that such problems bring.

▶ Children with ADHD require to be motivated and stimulated. Current research is examining the benefits of computer-assisted learning and is finding that this kind of input is holding the attention better than more traditional ways of inputting knowledge and understanding. Each child is different, and teachers have to adapt their teaching style and the learning environment to suit each child.

AUTISM AND ASPERGER'S SYNDROME

Autism is a very difficult condition to describe, because each autistic child or adult will demonstrate different aspects of the condition. The video produced by the National Autistic Society is called *The Problem Is*

Understanding, and that describes the plight of children who cannot understand the communication of others. They also lack the imagination to anticipate events and so make the necessary preparations and adjustments to carry them out.

Some children, often very good-looking, appear 'normal' until they are 2 or 3. They may have a large vocabulary and even enjoy poetry, but then regress, losing most or all of their language. This is devastating for their families. Many have prodigious memories; some have islets of brilliance, such as 'the 10 year old who can do A-level maths but can neither read nor wipe his bottom' (Moore 2004). Some do not speak at all. And so there is a spectrum of disability.

Higher-functioning autists are often named as having Asperger's syndrome. While they have communication difficulties based on not understanding what another person is thinking, they do not have the profound learning disabilities that are a feature of autism. They have obsessions, and these can result in high levels of expertise in specific areas that may benefit humanity – for example, research requiring careful protracted study. Alternatively, the obsessions, such as collecting bus tickets or sweet papers, may have no productive use at all. Children with Asperger's do have languages, although their communication can be stilted and inappropriate. They are often isolates.

Wing and Gould (1979) identified three features of autism: impairments of language and communication, impairments of flexibility of thought, and impairment of social interaction. These descriptors lead to the autistic child being seen as 'silent, aloof and withdrawn'.

Language and communication

- ► Children may have no language at all or use inappropriate language because they do not appreciate what another person is thinking.
- ► Use pronouns incorrectly – omission of 'I'.
- ► Avoid eye contact.
- ► Have no understanding of humour, sarcasm or idiom.
- ► Have 'relationships' only with those who do not pressurise or attempt to change routines.

Flexibility of thought

- ► Show lack of imaginative play (tied to the here and now).
- ► Have an obsession with detail and with collecting items.

129

▶ Exhibit only transitory imitation if any at all.

▶ Have poor planning, organisational and sequencing skills (these need anticipation of what is to come).

▶ Cannot transfer learning from one situation to another; skills are tied rather than habituated or generalised.

▶ Many autistic people are hypersensitive to environmental cues. Children do best in a quiet space with plain walls and carpets. Often children withdraw from bustle and noise, escaping into their own confined world. Smells, such as those of perfume, disinfectant or cooking smells, can distress them.

Social interaction

▶ Show lack of interest or attention to other people.

▶ Have no understanding of group interaction or social rules.

▶ Prefer isolation.

▶ Show little recognition of danger.

▶ Have no innate understanding of social rules, e.g. will spread excrement.

Moore (2004) explains that children should have the benefits of a special needs nursery as early as possible so that 'professionals can divert them from their rigid routines before they become stuck'. She is reinforcing the idea of critical learning times for these children.

DOWN'S SYNDROME

Down's syndrome is a congenital condition. It is rarely hereditary. Having Down's syndrome is the most common reason for learning disability (1 in every 700 live births per year). It is caused by the presence of an extra chromosome (three copies of no. 21 instead of two, and so is often called trisomy 21). The condition results in the children developing more slowly than their peers – a difference that widens with age. But the children do progress; there is no evidence of a plateau in their cognitive development if teaching is geared towards their strengths.

Children with Down's syndrome learn best in groups, and they use their peer group as models. Inclusion is important. The myth is that they are always happy and smiling, but this is not strictly true. It is true, however, that their social skills are generally higher than their academic ones. They often use hugs and cuddles to show affection, as well as to stop people asking them to learn things they do not wish to know! But they feel sad or distressed like any other child if they are not secure in a positive inclusive environment.

However, as the learning profile of a child with Down's syndrome is different from that of a child who has global developmental delay, an ordinary teaching programme taken at a slower pace is not adequate. Common impairments that can inhibit learning are:

▶ visual and auditory impairment;
▶ physical impairments and delayed motor skills;
▶ speech difficulties;
▶ poor short-term or working memory.

Visual impairment

Although children with Down's syndrome learn best visually and are able to access the curriculum most easily in this mode, 60–70 per cent require spectacles before they are 7 years old. Strategies to support the children include asking parents to have their child's vision checked, placing the child close to the teaching area, using large type on notices and providing large sheets of paper for paintings and drawings.

Hearing impairment

Many children have some level of hearing loss. Up to 20 per cent have a sensorineural loss caused by developmental defects in the ear and the auditory nerves. Upper respiratory infections are common, and these can result in glue ear. This prevents sensation penetrating into the smaller sinuses and ear canals. Hearing can fluctuate, and children who cannot hear well need to be differentiated from children who make the same response through not understanding rather than not hearing what has been said.

▶ Children with Down's syndrome should be near the front of the class.
▶ The teacher should speak directly to the child, making sure that non-verbal cues complement the spoken words.
▶ Using extra gestures can provide reinforcement.
▶ If another child answers, the teacher should repeat the key points so that the child does not miss out.

▶ The teacher should provide as much visual back-up material as possible, such as word banks, pictures from magazines and posters.

Physical development: poor gross and fine motor development

Most Down's children have been floppy babies with poor muscle tone and loose joints. As a result, they are late in achieving their motor milestones. Many are short in stature, and this may affect their liking for gross motor activities. The structure of the hand is different, making the pincer grip harder to achieve. Visual and auditory impairments combine to impair movements too.

Heart defects that can be corrected are relatively common, and the presence of such a defect may also prevent practice at the critical learning times.

Speech difficulties

Most children with Down's syndrome have delayed speech and language development but learn to communicate adequately at an early age. Vocabulary may be acquired slowly, so in the nursery it is important to use carefully chosen words and phrases to promote understanding. Some children have a small upper jaw, which may inhibit the movements that control articulation. Some children have very limited speech and depend on signing for communication. They are still likely to understand what is said.

A speech and language difficulty inevitably affects thinking and reasoning skills. Distractibility is another feature of Down's syndrome, and all these combine to prevent abstract thinking and problem-solving.

Behaviour difficulties

There are no behaviour difficulties associated with Down's syndrome, but, of course, tiredness due to the extra effort that has to be made to learn and low self-esteem may cause frustration to spill over and cause the child to be sad.

Children with Down's syndrome are strong visual but poor auditory learners. They need visual materials to help them learn. So reading, where the print makes the sound visual, is a curriculum area where

Down's children can often excel, and this is critical to accessing all areas of the curriculum. The key message is that these children have a specific learning profile, not just developmental delay.

DYSPRAXIA

Dyspraxia is a difficulty with planning and carrying out efficient and effective movements. It thus affects every aspect of learning and coping, both at home and at school. Timing skills are affected, which, for example, makes getting on to an escalator difficult, and actions that happen at the midline of the body are also very difficult to carry out. So, academically average or bright children with dyspraxia cannot fasten buttons or do up zips. They find writing very difficult because of lack of strength in the fingers and arms. A poor sense of balance means that things children want to be able to do, such as kicking a ball or riding a bike or using a skateboard, are achieved only with intensive practice. But achieved they can be.

One of our Scottish youngsters with dyspraxia, Grant, has just won an international award for judo. He explained, 'Well, all my life I've been falling over and I've learned to get up quickly . . . really learning to bounce. So I chose a sport where that would help. And it did!'.

While the term 'dyspraxia' is most often used in education, the diagnostic and statistical manual (DSM–IV) of the American Psychiatric Association uses the term 'developmental co-ordination disorder' (DCD), and provides the following indicators:

▶ There is a marked impairment in the development of motor co-ordination.
▶ The impairment significantly interferes with academic achievement or activities of daily living.
▶ The difficulties are not due to a medical condition such as cerebral palsy, hemiplegia or muscular dystrophy.
▶ It is not a pervasive developmental disorder.
▶ If developmental delay is present, the motor difficulties are in excess of those usually associated with it.

What does this mean for children in the nursery? Most children with dyspraxia have been floppy babies, and this lack of strength means that their motor milestones are achieved just within the 'normal' time limit. They rarely crawl, because they lack the cross-lateral co-ordination to

133

make crawling possible. This difficulty impacts on their balance and spatial decision-making too, because children who crawl learn to balance on all fours in a safe position. Then they learn to adjust their weight as they reach out or move forward.

Poor muscle tone can affect articulation, chewing and swallowing, and if it affects the bladder, then wet pants happen every day. With older children, poor organisational skills hamper their progress, although timetables and realistic goals (which can be highly academic) help a lot. This is a hidden handicap, and, sadly, one that can prevent some children getting the support they require.

DYSLEXIA

Dyslexia is a difficulty with processing information. It is a complex condition, with different children having a different set of difficulties – although they do cluster around reading and spelling. Added to those are difficulties in organisation and sequencing, understanding of time – for example, how long something takes – and a poor working memory.

Magnetic resonance imaging shows that people with dyslexia have differences in the arrangement of magnocells in the brain. Dyslexia is genetic, although older members of the family who have had difficulties learning to read and spell may not have been diagnosed.

Mears–Irlen syndrome is a different condition to dyslexia, although it too affects reading and written spelling. Children with this condition see letters on the page move or blur, causing eye strain and avoidance of reading. Coloured overlays can help. These have to be obtained through an optician, but they are effective and help reading in terms of both speed and accuracy.

Thus, there are many different difficulties that must be carefully observed, identified and given the right kind of support for as long as it takes. Communication with parents is critically important too, and must be one of the key goals for practitioners in the next years. Only then can the children fully benefit. Nothing could be more important, for after all, 'it is to the young that the future belongs'.

Appendix 1

List of competences

■ Lists of competences

Social development helps children:	Perceptual-motor development helps children:	Intellectual development helps children:	Emotional development helps children:
build relationships with others; learn from others; interact appropriately with adults and children; cooperate in group situations; take the lead role in decision-making; take the subsidiary role at times; learn to empathise, i.e. understand different perspectives; understand how events affect others; develop socially acceptable behaviour in different circumstances; make decisions (social and/or moral) and stay with them; appreciate the value of friendship; develop altruism, i.e. caring for others at some cost to oneself.	control their movements with increasing dexterity; move effectively and safely in different environments; develop spatial and kinesthetic awareness; develop the abilities that underlie skilled performance; know how to organise sequences of movement; become involved in health-giving activities; enjoy participating in sports, gymnastics and dance; be confident in tackling new movement challenges.	develop knowledge and understanding of the world; develop language and communication skills; develop the capacity to think logically and rationally; make informed decisions; develop mathematical and scientific concepts solve problems; think creatively about new ways of doing things; concentrate on the task at hand; cope with specialised learning in the classroom and at home.	approach new situations with confidence; express feelings and emotions; pretend to be someone else cope with anxieties and be more resilient; enjoy open-ended problems; appreciate works of art/music/dance; become aware that others have needs too; cry if they want to; understand the perception of other people; develop altruism; appreciate the atmosphere in, say, a church; be innovative and imaginative.

Source: Based on Scottish Executive Education Department, *The Early Intervention Programme: Raising Standards in Literacy and Numeracy*, annual report, 1999.

The adventures of Millie and Maurice Mouse down the hole!

Mrs Mouse put on her best pink hat and called to her children, 'Maurice and Millie, do come quickly, it's time to go to nursery, and you must look smart on your very first day. Come and let me see. Oh Millie, your whiskers are still all milky from breakfast – go and wash at once'. But instead of washing, Millie wiped her long whiskers with her new hanky specially bought for nursery, and soon it was grubby and sticky. 'What a naughty girl,' said Mrs Mouse, 'no cheese for you today . . . and where's your brother? I hope he's not up to mischief too? Where is that boy?'.

'He's under his bed,' said Millie. 'Under his bed, under his bed,' said Mrs Mouse. '**Whatever is he doing there?**'. 'He doesn't want to go to nursery,' said Millie; 'he's frightened that the big mice will chase him!' 'What nonsense,' said Mrs Mouse. 'I am really getting very cross! I have two silly children today. What am I going to do?' She shook her head so hard that one of the cherries from her best pink hat broke off and rolled right over the floor and down a tiny hole. 'Oh no,' cried Mrs Mouse, 'my best pink hat is spoiled. What am I to do?'. And at that she sat down, put her paws over her eyes and cried and cried!

Millie decided to help. 'Maurice, come here at once,' she cried. 'You must find the cherry from Mum's hat – it's gone under the floor!'. 'Under the floor,' said Maurice, '**Whatever is it doing there?**'. 'Make yourself very tiny,' urged Millie, 'and squeeze down the hole to find it!'. 'What, go down there?' cried Maurice. 'But it's dark, and what if I get lost?' Millie jumped up and down. 'Go on, go on,' she cried. 'There's no time to waste! You must be brave, for poor Mum is very upset. I'll bring a torch and then you'll see the cherry. You won't disappear, for I'll hold on to your tail as well'.

'Well all right,' said Maurice, 'but don't let go, for there could be all sorts of things down there – maybe even a snake or a ghost!'. So poor Maurice squeezed down into the hole while Millie held on to his tail. 'Shine the torch,' yelled Maurice. 'I think I see something moving, but don't pull my tail so hard – oh! oh! oh! you've nearly pulled it off!'. Millie got such a fright that she let go of both Maurice's tail and the torch. He rolled head over heels far down the hole! The torch went out too. Poor, poor Maurice!

Meantime, Mrs Mouse had dried her tears and and put her best pink hat safely back in the wardrobe. 'Now', she said, 'I'll have to save up all my money to buy a new red cherry for my hat. No pocket money for you children today, I'm afraid. And we'll have to leave for nursery now or we'll miss the bus. Where is that boy?'. Millie took a deep breath and pointed to the skirting board. 'He's down that hole,' said Millie. 'Down that hole,' shrieked Mrs Mouse, 'Oh no! **Whatever is he doing there?** U, u, u, u!'.

Under the floor, where it was spooky and dark, Maurice met a large black beetle sitting on a stone rubbing his leg. 'Guess what,' said Mr Beetle angrily, 'I was just out for a stroll when this huge boulder came hurtling down the path and banged into my leg. Look, it's all bruised and sore. It could even be broken!'. Maurice was horrified, but he had to explain. 'That wasn't a boulder,' whispered Maurice hastily, 'it was only a cherry from my Mum's best hat!'. 'A cherry, a cherry,' exclaimed Mr Beetle, '**Whatever is it doing there?**'. 'It's not a real cherry – I have to take it back to Mum,' explained Maurice, 'and then she'll sew it back on her hat and be happy again'. 'Oh no you don't,' said Mr Beetle grumpily, 'anything that comes into this hole is mine! I'll put that cherry into my garden shed right now!'. What was poor Maurice to do?

At that very moment, Millie shone the torch right down into the hole, right where the cherry lay. Suddenly it glowed in the dark. 'It's on fire,' shouted Mr Beetle, 'it's on fire. Get it out of here before it burns my house down.' But the cherry was muddy and all covered with dirt, and no matter how hard poor Maurice tried, he could hardly push it up the slope – for he was just a little mouse!

When Mrs Mouse and Millie heard all the commotion, they ran to fetch Mr Mouse, who was busy gathering ears of corn for lunch. 'Come quickly,' they cried, 'Maurice is down that hole!'. 'Down that hole!' exclaimed Mr Mouse. '**Whatever is he doing there?**'. And he pushed his head and shoulders into the hole to see! 'Oh Dad, it's great to see you,' cried Maurice. 'Take a hold of the cherry – quickly, quickly before it rolls back down the hole again'. Mr Mouse grasped the cherry in his two front paws, but when he tried to back out of the entrance to the hole, he found that he was stuck! Mrs Mouse and Millie just didn't know what to do. They pulled his tail as hard as they could, but he didn't budge – not one centimetre!

'Fetch the neighbours,' cried Mrs Mouse. 'Go at once and tell them that your Dad is stuck fast in a hole . . . and Maurice is down there too. Oh dear, oh dear, what a day this is turning out to be!!'. Luckily the neighbours came running in. 'Goodness me,' they cried. '**Whatever are they doing there?**'. They pulled and pulled and pulled again, and suddenly Mr Mouse, Maurice and the cherry all plopped out and everyone started to laugh and clap. 'You are a brave mouse after all,' said Mrs Mouse as she gave both children a hug. 'You can't be afraid to go to nursery now!'.

And when they got there, Millie and Maurice told all the other children about their adventure, but nobody mentioned that both Mr Mouse and Maurice had very sore tails!

Bibliography

Afasic Scotland (2000) *Glossary Sheets*. Dundee: Scottish Executive.

Atkin, J., Bastiani, J. and Goode J. (1988) *Listening to Parents: An Approach to the Improvement of Home–School Relations*. London: Croom Helm.

Attwood, T. (1998) *Asperger's Syndrome: A Guide for Parents and Professionals*. London: Jessica Kingsley.

Ayres, J. (1972) *Sensory Integration and Learning Disorders*. Los Angeles: Western Psychological Services.

Bastiani, J. (1992) *Working with Parents*. London: NFER-Routledge.

Bee, H. (2001) *The Developing Child*. London: HarperCollins College Publishers.

Bowerman, M. (1985) Beyond communicative adequacy: From piecemeal knowledge to an integrated system in the child's acquisition of language. In K.E. Nelson (ed.) *Children's Language*. Hillsdale, NY: Erlbaum, vol. 5, pp. 369–398.

Burnett, E. and Frame, J. (2003) *Speech and Language Difficulties in the Early Years*. Edinburgh: Lothian University Hospitals NHS Trust.

Case, R. (1985) Cited in Smith, P., Cowie, H. and Blades, M. (2002) *Understanding Children's Development*, 3rd edn. Oxford: Blackwell.

Cohen, D. (1996) *The Development of Play*. London: Croom Helm.

Craig, G. (2002) *Information on ADHD*. Edinburgh: North West Edinburgh ADHD Pilot Project.

Department for Education and Employment (DfEE) (2000) *Curriculum Guidance for the Foundation Stage*. London: Qualifications and Curriculum Authority.

Elkind, D. (1991) Academic pressures too much too soon: The demise of play. In E. Klugman and S. Smilansky (eds) *Children's Play and learning: Perspectives and Policy Implications*. New York: Teachers College Press, pp. 3–17.

Family Numeracy Project (1998) *Involvement with Parents*. Edinburgh: General Teaching Council.

Foley, M.A., Wilder, A., McCall, R. and Van Vorst, R. (1993) The consequences for recall of children's ability to generate interactive imagery in the absence of external supports. *Journal of Experimental Psychology* 56, 173–200.

Garner, P. and Gains, C. (2000) The debate that never happened. *Special – The Official Magazine of NASEN*.

Goddard, S. (2002) *Reflexes, Learning and Behavior: A Window into the Child's Mind*. Eugene, OR: Fern Ridge Press.

Green, D., Henderson, S., Barnett, A. and Baird, G. (2000) The clumsiness in children with developmental co-ordination disorder and Asperger's syndrome – same or different? In Conference proceedings of *'Stepping Forward'*. Hitchen, UK: Dyspraxia Foundation.

Harris, P. (1992) *Children and Emotion: The Development of Psychological Understanding*. Oxford: Blackwell.

House, R. (2002) The central place of play in early learning and development. *The Mother* no. 2, Summer, pp. 44–46.

Isaacs, S. (1930) *Intellectual Growth in Young Children*. London: Routledge and Kegan Paul.

Isaacs, S. (1933) *Social Development in Young Children*. London: Routledge and Kegan Paul.

Kail, R. (1990) *The development of Memory in Children*, 3rd edn. New York: Freeman.

Kaplan, B., Dewey, D.M., Crawford, S.G. and Wilson, B.M. (2001) The Term co-morbidity is of questionable value in reference to developmental disorders: Data and theory. *Journal of Learning Disabilities* 34, 555–565.

Keen, D. (2001) Specific neurodevelopmental disorders. Paper presented at the Conference on the Needs of Children with Specific Developmental Difficulties, Bishop Auckland, UK, March.

Macintyre, C. (2002) *Play for Children with Special Needs*. London: David Fulton.

Macintyre, C. and Deponio, P. (2003) *Assessing and Supporting Children with Specific Learning Difficulties: Looking beyond the Label to Assess the Whole Child*. London: Routledge.

Macintyre, C. and McVitty, K. (2003) *Planning the Pre-5 Setting*. London: David Fulton.

Macintyre, C. and McVitty, K. (2004) *Movement and Learning in the Early Years*. London: Sage/Paul Chapman.

McLean, A. and Brown, J. (1992) Developing a support service for children with social, emotional and behavioural difficulties. In G. Lloyd (ed.) *Chosen with Care? Response to Disturbing Behaviour.* Edinburgh: Moray House Publications.

Main Report (2003) *Moving to Mainstream.* Prepared by Audit Scotland in partnership with HMI.

Moore, C. (2004) *George and Sam.* London: Viking (Penguin).

Rapin, I. and Allen, D.A. (1987) *Developmental Dysphasia and Autism in Pre-school Children: Proceedings of the First International Symposium on Speech and Language Disorders in Children.* London: Afasic.

Rawson, M. and Rose, M. (2002) Ready to Learn: From Birth to School Readiness. Stroud: UK, Hawthorn Press.

Scottish Consultative Council on the Curriculum (1999) *A Curriculum Framework for Children 3–5.* Edinburgh: SCCC.

Scottish Executive (2003) *The Child at the Centre.* Edinburgh: Scottish Office.

Scottish Executive Education Department (1999) *The Early Intervention Programme: Raising Standards in Literacy and Numeracy.* Annual report.

Serfontein, G. (1996) *The Hidden Handicap.* Sydney: Simon and Schuster.

Tree House Trust (2004) *The Invisible Disability.* General Teaching Council (Scotland), March (www.treehouse.org.uk).

UNESCO (1996) *Legislation Pertaining to Special Educational Needs.* Paris: UNESCO.

Wing, L. and Gould, J. (1979) Severe impairments of social interactions and associated abnormalities: epidemology and classification, *Journal of Autism and Developmental Disorders* 9, 11–29.

Woolfendale, S. (1992) *Empowering Parents and Teachers.* London: Cassell.

Index